Christians and Communists

An ecumenical perspective

Ans J. van der Bent

THE
RISK
BOOK
SERIES

World Council of Churches, Geneva

Cover design: Paul May
ISBN No. 2-8254-0665-1
© 1980 World Council of Churches,
150, route de Ferney, 1211 Geneva 20, Switzerland
No. 9 in the Risk book series

Table of contents

Introduction

A number of concerns come together in the publication of this ecumenical guidebook on Communism, socialism, and the Christian faith.

As librarian of the World Council of Churches, I have been privileged over the years to talk with many visitors to the Ecumenical Centre in Geneva and to encounter the ideas of many other observers whose writings have crossed my desk. These contacts have frequently raised serious questions about the stance of the WCC on important social issues in the contemporary world. Those who have been critical — often themselves sympathetic supporters of the vision of the unity of the Body of Christ in the world — have sometimes asked whether the WCC, particularly during the past decade or so, has not been engaged in systematically "politicizing" the Christian faith. More outspoken opponents have charged from time to time that WCC thinking is a revolutionary doctrine indistinguishable in its aims and strategies from Marxism.

There are varying degrees of misunderstanding and misrepresentation involved in these critiques. But rather than dismiss out of hand all the concerns raised in this context, I believe that the time has come to attempt an overview of these vitally important political and social issues, to review — or perhaps in some cases introduce — the history that explains the shape of the encounter between Christians and Marxists in the world today, and to stimulate further thinking on the responsibilities in society and politics which Christians take on when (in the words of the WCC Basis adopted in 1948) we "confess the Lord Jesus Christ as God and Saviour" and "seek to fulfil together our common calling to the glory of the one God, Father, Son, and Holy Spirit."

Handbooks on this subject for church groups, students, and individual Christians are surprisingly rare. Longer and more scholarly studies of specific issues and developments in Marxism have continued to appear through the years; and a number of these are mentioned in the select bibliography at the end of this guide. And there has been no shortage of Christian "anti-Communist" literature; most of it frankly propagandistic and, as we shall see in more detail in

Chapter Three, founded on an oversimplified view of the world in absolute terms of darkness and light. But the few available books that do seek to introduce these issues to a more general Christian readership date back fifteen years or more, view things from an inevitably North American perspective (that is where several of them were written), and reflect the particular Cold War situation of the time in which they were written. It is this gap which the present book is meant to fill.

For some readers the term "guidebook" may suggest something like the owner's manual for a new car, specifying what the user *must* do if things are to work properly. The aim of this book is much more modest: it is rather a "guide" in the sense of a map of the terrain. Often the first step toward understanding something is recognizing how complex it is. In the case of Marxism and socialism, many Christians have skipped this critical step. They have failed to recognize how Marxists and socialists, separated by time and distance and circumstance, may vary enormously in their analyses of social and political structures, the degree of their convictions, and their dedication to the radical change of society.

At the outset we shall introduce briefly the teachings of Karl Marx and his followers. It will become apparent that some of Marx's most challenging ideas do not form part of Communist theory today. Leninism, Stalinism, and Maoism represent different historical developments and applications of Marxist principles. We shall see in Chapter Two how the claims and promises both of capitalism and of socialism and Communism to mark the way to a more just and humane society have fallen far short of realization in the contemporary world.

Chapter Three will offer a look at several options for working out the relationship between Christianity and Marxism: doctrinaire anti-Communism, dialogue between Christians and Marxists, and Christian socialism. A consideration of these three movements will make it evident that none of them has yet emerged as a realistic and satisfactory model for alleviating the ideological conflicts of today's world. The issues will not, however, disappear; and in

Chapter Four we shall look in particular at how the ecumenical movement is inevitably confronted with them. In the scope of this short guidebook, of course, we cannot undertake a complete review of the involvements of the WCC, much less of the ecumenical movement as a whole. Instead, we shall focus on representative developments in the WCC as they have emerged in the work of the Faith and Order Commission, the Programme to Combat Racism, and the recent overall programme emphasis on a "just, participatory, and sustainable society."

Building on these concerns, we conclude in Chapter Five with a look at some of the ways in which these ecumenical ideals are brought down to earth in the political involvements of Christians in their home churches. As in the rest of the book, the focus here will not be — indeed, *cannot* be — on specifying right and wrong political choices and strategies. Instead, our attempt will be to sketch some of the challenges facing Christians who are committed to the improvement of human life for all the people of the world.

Those who want quick answers and ready-made formulas will not find them in these pages. For too long we have allowed slogans and caricatures — whether it be "Workers, unite!" and "Power to the people!" or the apocalyptic condemnation of Marxism as demonic and atheistic tyranny, the anti-Christ whose appearance promises the immediate and triumphant return of Christ on the clouds — to take the place of a tough-minded and critical engagement with the forces that operate in the world today.

As champions of the freedom of conscience, religious liberty, and the rights of the poor and the exploited and powerless, Christians must become more sensitive to the ideals they share with Marxism. In the process they will become more aware of their own shortcomings as well as the signal failures of Marxists to realize their aims. Such an understanding — to which the present book aims to make its own modest contribution — will in fact result in a deeper insight into God's ultimate design and destiny for humanity.

Obviously, a book of this length cannot treat its subjects in great detail. It is hoped that interested readers will be led to pursue in greater depth the topics introduced here, using the resources mentioned in the bibliography and other available literature, but also through personal and communal reflection on and engagement in the issues of our day.

* * *

I am indebted to several colleagues in the Ecumenical Centre in Geneva for their valuable suggestions and pertinent criticisms, and I wish to thank in particular several colleagues in the World Council Department of Communication for their assistance and encouragement throughout the process from typescript to published book.

I.   The story of Communism

Karl Marx

Propagandist, pamphleteer, revolutionist, organizer of labour movements, scholar — Karl Marx was undeniably one of the pivotal figures in the history of the world. Whatever we may think of the accuracy or inaccuracy of his analysis of society's ills, no matter how we may evaluate the solutions he proposed, we cannot afford to ignore him and his legacy. From the beginning, unfortunately, all too many Christians have tried to do just that.

In this opening chapter we shall take a quick look at 150 years of history. Our focus will be on how Marxism has developed over the years, particularly in the two great world powers in which the Communist Party holds the reins of government — the Soviet Union and China. Too often we treat Marxism as a phenomenon which appeared full-blown some time after World War II. But it is an *emerging* system, and has been for a century and a half. From the perspective of history some of the events which form the stuff of today's headlines may one day be seen as important turning points; others may prove to have been insignificant detours with no lasting consequences. Although we have no sure way now of distinguishing between them, it is helpful to bear in mind this reality of change and development in Marxism.

Who was Marx? He was born on May 5, 1818, of Jewish parents (who were subsequently baptized as Protestants) in the Prussian city of Trier. He studied at the Universities of Bonn and Berlin and at 23 received a doctorate from the University of Jena. His marriage to Jenny von Westphalen, the daughter of a high government official, was one of deep love that withstood the vicissitudes of all the subsequent years. Several of Marx's children died in childhood, including his only son Edgar.

His reputation as a radical came early, and he lived in exile in Paris and Brussels before moving to London in 1849, where he spent the rest of his life, most of it in dire poverty. In spite of frequent setbacks and persistent illness, he was a prolific writer. The *Communist Manifesto*, jointly written by Marx and Friedrich Engels in 1848, summarizes his whole social philosophy. The only important organiza-

Karl Marx

tional activity Marx ever undertook was his leadership of the International Workingmen's Association (the First International), beginning in 1864. His own followers were a minority among the members. The International declined, and conflict with anarchists put an end to it. Marx died in 1883, the year after his wife's death.

Marx was a true child of his time. While he was writing and researching his *Capital* in the solitude of the British Museum library, he was well aware of the alarming consequences of rapidly advancing industrialization all around him in Great Britain. The despair and oppression that were the lot of the exploited men, women, and even children on whose backs the system was being constructed, but who enjoyed none of its benefits, were intimately familiar to him. No other philosopher of the second half of the nineteenth century shared Marx's insights into this tragedy nor his radical commitment to change the plight of these workers.

As a child of his time Marx remained an advocate of the idealism and optimism of his century. His aim was to liberate people from the pressure of economic needs so that they could be more fully human. Of course he had no way of knowing how the next century would differ in fundamental ways from his own. A question for those who seek to examine critically and objectively the achievements of Marxism in the twentieth century is how far Marx's followers have remained true to Marx's original utopian expectations and how far they have sacrificed these in the interest of hard political realism.

Marx himself summarized his teaching in three brief points:

1. The existence of classes in society is linked only with specific historical phases in the development of production.

2. The necessary outcome of the struggle between the classes in society is the "dictatorship of the proletariat" — the working class.

3. The dictatorship of the proletariat is only a transitional stage before the abolition of all classes and the rise of a classless society.

The story of how these theoretical-sounding propositions have taken hold and have been modified and extended in the lives of millions of people is the substance of much of the history of the past century and a half. In the pages that follow in this chapter, too, we shall be discussing ideas. The blood and tears, the bitter struggles, victories, and defeats which individuals and groups and parties have experienced, the human stories — these must be told elsewhere. Our purpose here is the more limited one of stimulating thought about the relationship of the Christian faith and the Christian church to this powerful contemporary reality. Yet it would be a serious mistake to approach this as a mere intellectual exercise.

Influences on Karl Marx

No matter how original and creative a thinker may be, it is possible to detect currents of earlier thought in a person's ideas and writings. Marx is no exception. In his work we can particularly trace the influences of German philosophy, British political economics, and French socialism. Marx did not simply take up their ideas into his system; in many cases he gave them a new slant or reacted strongly against them.

It was the German idealist philosopher Georg W. F. Hegel (1770-1831) from whom Marx derived the "dialectical" sense that history is a continuous process — that it moves forward toward a goal through the clash of movements and the resulting formation of new historical forces. But as Marx saw things, Hegel's idealism stood reality on its head. For Marx, it is the material, not the ideal, which is the true reality. And in its economic manifestation this material reality is the key to understanding all social institutions.

Marx's inhospitable attitude to religion is well-known. He was familiar with the explosively anti-religious writings of Bruno Bauer (1809-1882) and Ludwig Feuerbach (1804-1872). According to Bauer, the Christian gospels are not a record of history but an account of human fantasies that grew out of people's emotional needs. There had never been an historical Jesus. Although sympathetic with Bauer's flatly atheistic position, Marx considered his view that society could be changed by changing people's minds as a basically reactionary idea.

Feuerbach's major work *The Essence of Christianity* was an effort to do theology in a thoroughly human fashion. Man is his own object of thought, Feuerbach said, and religion is merely the human consciousness of the infinite. What this did was reduce God to the outward projection of inner human nature. Feuerbach's influence on Marx was strong, but the often-quoted remark from his *Theses on Feuerbach* that "the philosophers have only interpreted the world in various ways: the point, however, is to change it" shows that launching a merely theoretical attack on religious belief was not a high priority for Marx.

In fact, Marx considered religion to be a symptom of what was wrong with society, not the problem itself. To attack Christianity directly would only inflame it. Marx was far more interested in getting to what he thought is the root problem: the economic ills of society. And so the key to Marx's atheism is a Yes to the world and to the mastery of human life and history rather than a No to religion and God. The road to self-liberation for the proletariat could be traveled only apart from a church whose clergy vied with each other for a piece of the action while urging the members to bear up patiently under oppression in the hope of a better life hereafter.

The names of the English political economists Adam Smith (1723-1790) and David Ricardo (1772-1823) appear frequently in *Capital*, Marx's major work. Indeed, the "labour theory of value" — the idea that labour alone is the ultimate real standard by which to measure the value of any commodity — was first formulated not by Marx (as is often thought) but by Adam Smith. Ricardo's classical economics, viewed through Marx's dialectical method, demonstrated that bourgeois society, like every social organism, must follow an inevitable path of development. In due course, capitalism would die and another, higher society would take its place.

Marx's attacks on the French socialist thinkers of the eighteenth and nineteenth centuries were based on careful study of their works, and their influence on him was pronounced. The idea of class struggle, for example, came from Louis de Saint-Simon (1675-1755) and Jean-Charles Sismondi (1773-1842). The well-known motto "from each according to his ability, to each according to his need" was taken over from Louis Blanc (1811-1882).

The French socialist Pierre-Joseph Proudhon (1809-1865) had tried to preserve the best features in economic institutions while eliminating the bad. Marx dismissed such efforts to unite the best in competition with the best in monopolies as a typical petty bourgeois failure to grasp the underlying laws of history. Instead of this "utopian socialism," which sought to work for human and social improvement, what is needed is a "scientific socialism," built on solid philosophical foundations and well grounded in the way things really are. This Marx sought to provide.

Developments in the 20th Century

During his lifetime Marx's influence was not great. It was only after his death that the growing International Workers' Movements increased it. Much of this can be attributed to the tireless efforts of Friedrich Engels (1820-1894), who devoted himself to editing the notes for the last two volumes of *Capital* and writing interpretative articles on Marx's philosophical theories.

Between 1883 and 1917 Marxism made a deep penetration, first into the social democracies of German-speaking countries and then into Latin and Slavic countries. In the twentieth century it was revived by the Russian leader Vladimir I. Lenin (1870-1924). Marxism as Lenin developed and applied it became the core of the theory and practice of Bolshevism and the Third International. Its triumph in overthrowing the Czarist government and elevating the Soviet Union to a position among the world's great powers is one of the key events that shaped the world of the twentieth century.

Lenin was probably the greatest revolutionist in the annals of human history. Though a disciple of Marx, he did far more than merely repeat the master's conclusions. Dialectic for him always had to lead back and forth, from reflection to activity and from activity to reflection. Lenin's first major contribution to Marxist theory was the concept of the party. This is the vanguard of professional revolutionaries — intellectuals and organizers — who represent the interests of the masses and will lead them toward the building of a new society. The meaning of Marx's idea of a "dictatorship of the proletariat" changed from the notion of a vast majority ruling over a tiny minority to that of an élite and carefully chosen party controlling a large majority. Lenin somewhere described socialism as "Soviet power plus electrification." In other words, socialism, having won political power in a backward and rural country, needed to produce its own industrial revolution.

Lenin's second major contribution was his thorough examination of the enemy. It is to him that we owe the theory of "imperialism as the highest stage of capitalism." What he called a "workers' aristocracy" had arisen in the industrial states. Corrupted by high wages, the workers themselves became participants in the exploitation of colonies. Thus the socialist revolution had to be made on the periphery of the global capitalist system, breaking it like a chain at its weakest link.

A struggle for power in the Soviet Union followed the death of Lenin. The victor was Joseph Stalin (1879-1953), a man whom Lenin had once recommended for removal from any position of authority. Stalin's ideas, under the name of Marxism-Leninism, constitute the doctrine of the European Communist Parties. He pursued the development of the Soviet Union with great vigour and ruthlessness. By practicing Marxism he assimilated it — and at the same time over-simplified it. Marx had linked the development of society with the development of the forces of production, and he had seen the intellectual enrichment of the working class as one result of common action and reflection. Stalin's perspective differed sharply: he believed that actions are to be judged not by what they intend to achieve, but solely in terms of what they do in fact objectively signify at the end of each historical period.

Not long after Stalin's death his policies came under sharp attack by Soviet leaders. At the 20th Congress of the Communist Party of the Soviet Union held in 1956, Nikita S. Khrushchev (1894-1971) charged that Stalin had fostered a "cult of the individual," centred on himself, which had led to one-man rule and "loathsome adulation" of Stalin's role as revolutionist, military leader, and scientific genius. Stalin was accused of falsifying facts in order to magnify his image and of arresting, deporting, and executing thousands of people without proper trial. After Khrushchev's death, this "de-Stalinization" gradually gave way in the 1970s to a campaign to rehabilitate Stalin's reputation, particularly stressing his military leadership during World War II.

Leonid I. Brezhnev (born 1906) has devoted considerable attention to curtailing ideological dissidence within the USSR and the satellite nations. A vivid example of this was the invasion of Czechoslovakia in 1968 by Warsaw Pact forces in response to what was seen as too much liberalization of the Communist system of government and party control under the leadership of Alexander Dubcek. Again, the 1980 incursion of the Soviet army into Afghanistan, overwhelmingly condemned in the United Nations, has been a matter of grave international concern. In the face of such events, it is deeply ironic to read the words of Marx ("A people which enslaves others forges its own chains''), Engels (''It is impossible for a victorious proletariat to force any kind of happiness on a foreign nation without undermining its own victory''), and Lenin himself (''If one day Finland, Poland, or the Ukraine detach themselves from Russia, this is not a bad thing . . . . No nation can be free if it oppresses other nations'').

Dissident movements in the Soviet Union today exert some impact on the system, but it is difficult to measure how much. These movements differ greatly from each other in character and aim. The so-called neo-Slavophiles are extremely critical of present-day Communism and wish to return to the religious and national traditions of pre-Bolshevist Russia. Patriotism, love of the soil and of work, an austere life-style, and the truth and solidarity of the Orthodox faith are among their chief emphases. The ''ethical socialists'' are anti-technocratic regarding both state capitalism in the East and liberal capitalism in the West. The ''democratic nationalists'' go even further, calling for the decolonization of the multinational Russian state and the founding of independent national republics. More than 135 million non-Russians live in the Soviet Union; and the democratic nationalists resist the imposition of a Russified economy on these peoples. They champion human rights, including personal, religious, and social freedoms.

The most outspoken opponents of the Marxist system are the ''liberals.'' These dissidents, many of them well-known in the Western press, reject Marxism as a discredited ideology of the past which has no moral right to continue to exist. Although they would oppose the restoration of economic structures based on private capitalism, they want to see a multi-party democracy based on a parliamentary system. Many of these dissidents have been forced into harsh sufferings because of their willingness to express their opposition publicly.

The Chinese Road

When the Chinese emperor was dethroned in 1912, it marked the end of nearly four thousand years of successive imperial dynasties. Nine years later the Chinese Communist Party was founded; and after years of struggle against foreign influences and internal opposition, a new Communist regime, the People's Republic of China, was officially proclaimed on October 1, 1949. The development of Communism in the world's most populous country followed a different path from that of the Soviet Union. Some observers have argued that the Chinese Communists simply applied the party programme more ruthlessly than the Soviets, establishing in the process one of the world's most totalitarian regimes. Others counter that the rapid social and economic development of China's 900,000,000 people in a little over thirty years could not possibly have been dictated by sheer oppression and manipulation from Peking.

In any case, two facts cannot be ignored. First, the confrontation between China's aggressiveness, its traditionally messianic sense of nationalism, its sometimes almost hysterical fear of foreigners, and what China sees as betrayal and animosity on the part of the Soviet Union has grown to an explosive hostility which still seems too deeply seated for reconciliation. Second, the resurgence of China as a great and independent participant in the world of nations points toward a shaking of the foundations in the existing international order of our century.

There is no doubt that the architect of the new China was Mao Tse-Tung (1893-1976). Mao was not a Soviet puppet: his leadership of China was his own achievement, and the policies which guided the country until his death bore his stamp. Maoism is an attempt, independent of Soviet guidance, to interpret, actualize, and apply traditional Marxist dogma to the particular historical and sociological reality of China. Mao believed from the beginning that a socialist revolution in China could succeed only if it were based primarily on the poor peasant masses who gave the country its fundamental social structure. Since these peasants constituted eighty per cent of the total population, it was only through them that a radical revolution in society and the state could begin.

Not that Mao's party was a peasant party. Like the Bolshevists, they were an élite of professional revolutionaries from different levels of society. The use of the peasants to seize power was a pragmatic political decision. China lacked the heavy industry and mass production necessary for the establishment of socialism according to the classic Marxist scheme. Mao was convinced that these could be created by activating a social awareness in the masses. The Chinese had to behave mentally and ideologically in a way that would allow for the development of industry. Thus the present situation in China is the result of a total control of the entire population in their daily political, economic, social, religious, cultural, and intellectual life. In this effort state power has been used both to persuade and coerce: indoctrination, propaganda, and methods of self-criticism go hand in hand with judicial and extra-judicial police and military force.

The people's communes of China do not claim to be genuine Communism already. This is a striking difference from the Soviet view of the transformation from socialism to Communism. Soviet ideology speaks of socialism as having triumphed completely, with the successive stage of transition to Communism having arrived. In the Chinese people's communes, these differences merge with one another. They are neither socialism alone nor Communism already realized: all the elements of the past, the present, and the partially begun future are contained in them.

Such a scheme strikes the Soviet Marxists as ideological chaos. But for the Chinese, deprived for a century by foreign oppressors of progress and its technical benefits, it is an attempt by a people to become a modern industrial state and a prosperous society at all costs. And behind the whole project lies the will to recapture for this ancient culture the position of leadership in the world which the Chinese feel they deserve. All of this has not proceeded, of course, in a straight line. Some of the movements designed to achieve the ambitious goals Mao had set led to serious disruptions; and the self-criticism which Mao had said should be "like a spring breeze and a gentle rain" struck like more of a hurricane.

A basic change in Soviet doctrine over the years was the abandonment of Lenin's and Stalin's view that war between capitalist and socialist powers is inevitable. The likelihood of mutual annihilation through the use of nuclear weapons in any such war led people like Khrushchev to emphasize the possibility of "peaceful coexistence" between different social systems, although an intensive struggle would continue on the ideological and economic levels. Khrushchev's famous threat to the West, "We will bury you!", was a prediction of economic, not military, triumph. Maoists, on the other hand, deny that nuclear weapons alter the law of class struggle or that a lasting peace can occur while imperialism remains. The Kremlin policy of peaceful coexistence they regarded as an anti-Leninist, revisionist sellout of proletarian internationalism. The so-called "parliamentary road" is no substitute for proletarian revolution. National liberation movements in less-developed areas, working-class movements in capitalist countries, and the "socialist camp" must mutually support one another. China reacts strongly to what it sees as the Soviet Union's "patriarchal" concept of inter-party relations, its great power chauvinism, and its national egoism over against its fellow Communist-controlled countries.

Whether Mao's political theories, as worked out in the Chinese revolution, will prove to be a model for other countries facing the problems of underdevelopment or will be a source of rancour, dogmatic hair-splitting, and needless sacrifice, its achievements will stand as a landmark in history. And China's determined struggle against what it considers revisionism on the part of the Soviet Union might develop into a formidable trend to invigorate the challenge Marxism-Leninism poses to the free world.

Of course, the great question is whether the Chinese will find a way to avoid the impasse into which they believe the Soviet Union has fallen. Can they escape the anarchy of consumerism on one hand and regimentation on the other? Where will the inspiration come to break free of the ever-new élitist policies of the past and elevate the peasant masses in the countryside in order to construct an essentially egalitarian society?

These uncertainties are heightened by the passing of Mao from the scene. No one knows what will be the new balance of power, as the army, the young people, and the new consumers make their demands felt. The earliest indications seem to be of a victory for the forces of modernization and pragmatism over the champions of conservative party orthodoxy, and of a greater desire for truly collective leadership to replace the one-man totalitarianism installed by Mao. Even so, the process in China's one-party system could hardly be called democratic. Yet it may open up the country's vast, entrenched bureaucracy to new people who were not associated with Mao.

But many China observers question how much these changes can help truly revitalize a country that must still be classified among the world's poorer ones. And as industrialization proceeds and the economy becomes more and more sophisticated, another serious question is whether the rulers in Peking will be able to solve the vast problems that burden the countries which are already advanced and industrialized.

Capitalism

The belief that the contemporary generation is one of unusual division, confusion, and strife has been a common theme throughout history. Few would deny the appropriateness of applying to our own day the words Thomas Paine uttered during the American Revolution: "These are the times that try men's souls!" Whether or not today's desperate universal search for purpose and meaning and the widespread absence of hope and vision are more acute than in other eras, there is abundant reason to deny that either capitalism or socialism is functioning well in the modern world. There is more than enough evidence to contradict the rhetorical claims of both camps to be promoting a concern for more justice, greater equality, and lasting peace for all the peoples on this planet.

Capitalism created an affluent society, but as people enjoy the goods this affluence brings them they want more and more. In place of the once-cherished ideals of industriousness, frugality, and temperance, the beneficiaries of capitalist wealth now seek consumption, leisure, and self-indulgence. Even Christianity, which once stressed tomorrow, now seems to put the emphasis only on today. Individual diligence and postponed rewards have given way to immediate gratification. Wants have become needs. One economically measurable reflection of this is the decrease in personal savings in favor of spending now.

Since vocation, talent, and savings are stretched thin by the affluent life-style, people make more and more demands on their governments. As a result, welfare spending now vies with defense expenditures as the largest item in many national budgets. And these rapidly increasing social outlays threaten to slow the growth of national economies even further. In countries where state social policies have been pervasive and popular for many years, governments have recently moved to the centre in an effort to unwind what is called the "socialist muddle."

The solution to the problem of inflation is excruciatingly elusive. One clear factor is the escalating cost of energy; and many Western governments have made the Organization of Petroleum Exporting Countries (OPEC) the scapegoat for the entire problem of inflation, though increased energy prices constitute only about a third of the annual inflation rate. Whether alternative energy sources which are safe and economical can be found is a pressing question; unless and until they are, inflation seems as certain as death and taxes.

More and more one hears that living standards and expectations must be stabilized. Some have argued that a "no-growth" society is the inevitable alternative to the increasing and destructive acquisitiveness of the present order. But can a new post-capitalist society, chastened and disciplined, really be inaugurated — or would such a society prove hopelessly at odds with the free-market mechanisms of contemporary capitalism, which stimulate production and consumption of new goods and services?

The ultimate exporters of capitalism to the developing world are the multinational corporations. Seen from one angle, these institutions are among the greatest resources for transferring development, since they create a middle class in many countries by providing jobs, training technicians, grooming managers, and awarding contracts to local suppliers. Yet many have argued that they function more as plunderers; and host governments, particularly in the Third World, soon learn that multinational companies will quickly shift plants, jobs, and capital to another country if it means that they can extract a more favorable rate of return on their investments or pay out lower taxes. Nor do the investments of the multinationals in underdeveloped nations deliver their benefits to the large majority of the population of those countries.

The predicament of the developing countries is that they can never catch up with that twenty percent of the world's population which disposes of eighty percent of the world's goods and resources. The poorer countries owe $350 billion to international banks and powerful national institutions — and that staggering debt is likely to increase rather than decrease. Meanwhile, the industrial world reaps the advantages of the fact that more than ninety percent of all scientists and technologists live in developed nations, where their findings are converted into ever more advanced technical processes. And half of these researchers are working on the development of new weapons systems.

Nevertheless, apologists for capitalism continue to claim that, for all its faults, it is still far superior to socialism, which they dismiss as unrealistic and contrary to human nature. Capitalism has not pushed workers deeper into poverty, they argue, as Marx had predicted it would; instead, it has lifted the vast majority of labourers into the middle classes. Unions provide employees with an effective counterforce to the power of management; and in some countries, when economic malaise sets in, it is corporate profits that suffer more than the wages of workers, which are usually fixed by contract.

As we saw in the opening chapter, Marx's case for Communism drew a great deal from the pathetic conditions of the working class in nineteenth-century industries. To be sure, workers in the huge factories and offices of our day suffer hardships as well, even if these are not usually physical dangers. But many companies in the capitalist world, particularly in Japan and West Germany, have made significant efforts — more so than in much of the socialist world — to alleviate these conditions by creating a stronger sense of participation by the workers in their tasks and in the firm as a whole. These range from experiments at reducing monotony on the assembly line to profit-sharing plans and stock-purchase options which give the workers a share in the company.

The fundamental rationale of capitalism is that it promotes human freedom by limiting the power of the state and enhancing the rights of the individual. Every true democracy practices some version of capitalism because political freedom is impossible without a measure of economic freedom. Churchill may have had a point in saying that the inherent vice of capitalism is the unequal sharing of blessings, but he went on to add that the inherent vice of socialism is the equal sharing of miseries.

Communism
Socialism and Communism respond to this case for capitalism by pointing out that this vice of equally sharing the

world's miseries is in fact imposed on the majority of the world's population by the wildly disproportionate blessings which a small minority shares, however unequally. The claim that capitalism is the most creative and dynamic force in civilization is persuasive only to those who idolize the ambitious, aggressive, and selfish individual. And in the global village where we all live today, we cannot afford to cater to the excessive needs of such imposing individuals. We must recover the ideal of human community and social justice.

In many underdeveloped countries, it is argued, a strong socialist regime is the only way to cope with the problems of overpopulation, unemployment, underemployment, vast urban slums, agricultural backwardness, and the absence of the skilled people and resources necessary for building up industry. Surely if human existence worldwide is to be meaningful, the hungry must be fed, the poor sheltered, the sick and aged provided with medical care, and the masses educated.

Laudable intentions and lofty goals, indeed. Yet the performance of the socialist and Communist societies which have articulated these goals must be questioned. What would Karl Marx, who anguished over the alienation of his fellow human beings suffering through the nightmare of the Industrial Revolution, say if he could see the use to which his political theories have been put in the Soviet Union and its satellites? The widely accepted picture of Marx as a rigid dogmatist of crude materialism and total class warfare, the stern hero of totalitarianism, is a creation of Communists; and this stereotype thrives on widespread Western ignorance and falsification of what Marx actually taught and believed. Marx's materialism had nothing to do with an anti-spiritual wish for submission and uniformity. In exchanging the spirit of the Russian Revolution for a primitive and aggressive pseudo-religious messianism, Soviet Marxism has distorted Marx's humanist philosophy as it reflects on the harmony among people and between people and nature.

Socialism is not intended as just another route to the production of more and more material goods or to a more equal distribution of these goods. Its original vision was of a new society, one in which equality is real and not merely formal, one in which differences between city and country, mental and manual labour, industry and agriculture have been eliminated. Achieving that kind of society requires much more than technological and industrial progress. Marx protested that dehumanization and the estrangement of people from their environment were inherent in Western capitalism. But today's Communist regimes, with their system of conservative state capitalism, are just as dehumanizing, alienating their citizens, treating them as appendixes to machines, transforming them into things.

Socialism

In our criticism of Western capitalist countries and Eastern Communist regimes we should pause briefly to note some other models for society which have been proposed or put into effect. Whether any of these is capable of producing a realistic alternative remains to be seen.

A number of nations have advanced considerably in the direction of a social democracy with a mixed economy and elaborate schemes to enhance the welfare and health of their citizens. Perhaps the leader among such countries, both in terms of social welfare and economic stability, is Sweden. Despite certain inequities, the rights of Swedish citizens to social assistance are extensive. Compulsory health-insurance programs reimburse all but a small portion, of doctors' fees, hospital treatment costs, and medicines. All citizens, as well as foreigners who reside in Sweden for a certain period, benefit from the substantial national pension system. Children's allowances are paid for each child under 16, and every mother receives a stipend at the birth of each child. Unemployment insurance in Sweden is based on voluntary premiums, but it is subsidized by the state. Comprehensive school education is offered to all citizens, and there is a strong emphasis on adult education. Although the prospects for the Swedish economy are not presently as bright as in earlier years, its advantages in the world marketplace are still pronounced.

18

We should also mention the regional and world socialist movements, which number among their participants such statesmen and political leaders as Willy Brandt and François Mitterand, among others. Some years ago an independent commission on international development issues, chaired by former West German Chancellor Brandt, undertook an extensive study of the prospects for both the Northern and Southern Hemispheres. Many agreed that a ten-year plan, financed by the wealthy industrialized countries and OPEC, should be undertaken to build up agriculture and industry in the southern countries, enfranchising the mass of poor consumers in those lands and making them productive by giving

Willy Brandt

Marc van Appelghem

them steady work and a just reward for it. In this way new resources and new markets would be available to North and South alike, and the flesh and bones of a genuine alliance of productive interest could be put on the rhetoric of interdependence. The Brandt commission report, *North-South — A Programme for Survival*, was published at the beginning of 1980. In it the urgent problems of inequality in the world and the failure of the present economic systems are debated. The report proposes long-term reforms by the year 2000, priority programmes for the 1980s, and emergency action to avert an imminent world crisis.

A third model worth noting is that of socialist states in Africa, such as Tanzania, where the need has been recognized to build up socialism on such African traditions as communal land ownership, the egalitarian practices of tribal societies, and the networks between people that existed before colonial domination. There are few statesmen in the world today whose vision matches that of Julius Nyerere, who has observed that "the choice before the free states of the world... is not between peaceful change and no change. The choice is between peaceful change and conflict."

But having mentioned these three alternative models we are still faced with the question of how realistic is a hope based on any of them. Are the social democracies not bound to remain islands in the ocean of big power interest and warfare? Has the Socialist International not lost much of its earlier élan, with its political support increasingly fragmented? Is the African commitment to socialism really more than lip-service to an ideal, so that the only people who are really applauding Nyerere are academic audiences in Western countries?

World Conflicts

We should supplement this effort at a realistic analysis of the defects of capitalism, Communism, and socialism in the world today with an equally sobering analysis of world political trends and events. On the one side, the great international vision of the *Communist Manifesto* — "Workers of the world, unite!" — has fallen far short of realization. Quite the contrary. All over the world Communist parties are riven by bitterly competitive factions who differ sharply on questions of Communist dogma and tactics.

The keen interest shown a few years ago in the development of "Euro-Communism" has already receded. The only European Communist leader to endorse the Soviet Union's occupation of Afghanistan was the French chief Georges Marchais. The Communist Parties of Rumania, Yugoslavia, Spain, and Italy spurned an invitation to join in a recent Communist summit meeting in Paris orchestrated by Moscow and organized by Marchais and the former Polish party leader Edward Gierek; and the summit meeting itself failed to produce the hard-line unanimity the Soviet Union was looking for. In the previous chapter we mentioned some of the sources of the ongoing and serious conflict between the Communist Parties of the Soviet Union and of China. Needless to say, the Kremlin is irked by what it sees as flirting with Chinese leaders on the part of such European Communist Parties as those in Rumania, Yugoslavia, and Italy.

Fundamental problems plague the Atlantic community as well, despite its common commitment to democracy and its largely shared cultural heritage. For a long period after World War II it was the United States which led and Europe followed. No longer is that the case. The dilemma of differing national interests versus the need for common action will trouble the Atlantic community for years to come.

As a global superpower the US has worldwide interests, and this leads it to seek changes in the present global situation. The regional powers have more limited interests, and consequently they tend to try to live with the present predicament. On the one hand, the US looks to its European allies for loyal support in moments of great need; on the other hand, its judgment of what is a moment of great need may well differ from that of the Europeans, who see Afghanistan, for example, as a remote land whose problems ought not to be the cause of a new Cold War — much less a hot one. The Europeans complain that Washington is unsteady in its management of relationships between the US and the Soviet Union and that it has failed in general to set and execute an appropriate course in foreign policy. The US counters that the European community is burdened by a cumbersome system of consultation which prevents quick response to international challenges and US initiatives. As a result, the Soviet Union is encouraged in its encroachments on other weaker countries.

Against the background of these disunities, capitalist and Communist imperialism go on to threaten one another and the world, though the hope that sheer military power can solve the problems of the world is nonsense. Christian churches on both sides of this divide need to be continually sensitive to the dangers of making uncritical alliances with either. No longer is Christianity — East or West — in the position of privileged leadership it once enjoyed, and from which it failed to exercise the prophetic ministry it had. In adjusting to this reality, Christians in the West must avoid the danger of an impatient activism supported by only vague ideals, and Christians in the East must avoid making worship a private indulgence that includes no active concern for others.

III. Condemnation and rapprochement

We noted at the beginning of the first chapter that far too many Christians have simply ignored Marxism and disregarded the challenges it presents to the Christian faith. In this chapter we shall be looking at three types of Christians who have not ignored Marxism and at the responses they have made — anti-Communism, dialogue with Marxists, and Christian socialism.

Anti-Communism

For some Christians the question of how to relate to Marxism is easy to answer. Communism is a godless ideology which enslaves millions of people. Christians must therefore oppose it with a vigour for which the term "crusade" is not too strong. There can be no question of working together, no talk of common goals. Quoting Leo XIII's definition of Commumism as a "fatal plague which insinuates itself into the very marrow of human society only to bring about its ruin," Pope Pius XI, in his encyclical *Divini Redemptoris* (1937), told the faithful that "no one who would save Christian civilization may collaborate with it in any undertaking whatsoever." Such unequivocal anti-Communist sentiments have been echoed in hundreds of books and pamphlets and articles and radio broadcasts disseminated by Christians, Catholic and Protestant alike, throughout the Western world.

Many Christians who are exposed this sort of anti-Communist propaganda accept it unquestioningly and with the best of intentions. Those who produce such literature do not entertain a moment's doubt that their insights into human nature and world affairs are superior to those of any follower of Marx. They make no attempt to understand the honest and deep-rooted anti-religious feelings of thousands of Communists who simply cannot be convinced that Christian churches have been or can be engaged in the struggle for social and economic justice. Even if these anti-Communists are willing to admit the truth in some of the charges Marxists have lodged against the church, they are convinced that these are minor and correctable flaws. Once these lessons have been learned, the Marxist critique can be deflected; and one can go on living comfortably within Western society.

Typical of the anti-Communist crusaders is Richard Wurmbrand. A Lutheran pastor from Rumania, Wurmbrand spent considerable time in prison there. His headquarters is now in Glendale, California, from where he issues a steady stream of printed material which has a wide influence on audiences in the English-speaking world and has been translated into several other languages. The world of Wurmbrand and those like him is the stark and simple world of the Cold War, in which an Iron Curtain separates good from evil—the free countries from the Communist nations. What problems exist in Western society are explained as the result of endless and diabolical Communist plots. "You Can Trust the Communists," the title of one widely circulated anti-Communist broadside announces, ". . . to be Communists!" Never does one hear from these crusaders about the racial injustice, the colonial and neo-colonial oppression, the militarism, the wasteful disregard of natural and human resources which threaten Western society from within. Small wonder that Wurmbrand was received enthusiastically on a triumphal lecture tour in South Africa.

The churches in Communist countries, according to the standard anti-Communist view, are peopled by traitors to the cause of Christianity. The only genuine Christians are those in the so-called underground church, which is God's chosen weapon against the demonic theories and practices of Marxism. In the face of this, the West should break through the walls separating it from the East, send in zealous missionaries who are ready to face martyrdom, convert the Communists to Christ, and thereby extend — and save — the free world.

Wurmbrand is correct in calling attention to the serious restrictions which governments in the Soviet Union and other socialist countries place on Christian communities. Too many Western European and North American Christians seldom give a thought or prayer for their harassed and persecuted brothers and sisters in these lands. Yet history has shown time and again that the real threat to the church

Krokodil, Moscow

is not so much oppression from without as coldness within: absence of love for the enemy, lukewarm faith, arid and abstract debates about doctrine without any passion for the liberating power of the gospel, and an unbiblically narrow view of conversion and salvation as limited to individuals in their private lives. To confront that sort of danger, smuggling Bibles and missionaries is an ineffective and even counterproductive strategy. For many Christian anti-Communists, it is atheism against which the attack on Marxism must be targeted. They cannot conceive of atheism as a thoughtful alternative to religious faith; it is rather the proof that something fundamental in the heart and mind of the one who professes it is distorted. So basic is this defect in Marxists that their analysis of what is wrong with the way things are and any ideas they may have about how to build a better society must be rejected out of hand. The atheistic concept of man and the world is utterly immoral and subhuman; how then could a Marxist deal with truly human questions — much less find any answers? Those who reason this way have sometimes asked why the World Council of Churches, which funds a Programme to Combat Racism, does not undertake a similar Programme to Combat Atheism.

We saw in the first chapter that Marx himself, though a convinced atheist, did not consider it worthwhile to devote a great deal of energy to attacking religion as such. The core of his atheism was the claim that "man must now revolve about himself as his own true sun." The strength of this doctrine was that it cut off the human race from the possibility of having anywhere or anything outside of itself to turn to. When you stand naked before the historical facts, your options and powers are whatever you find them out to be, and it is no solution to project these options and powers onto some realm outside of history.

When astronaut Gagarin returned from his first space flight, Party Secretary Nikita Khrushchev asked him whether he had seen God. Gagarin's reply: "No God."

It is at this point that a rigorous engagement between Christian faith and Marxist atheism must take place. Only when all realities are taken seriously in their own proper authority, autonomy, and strength — and that includes the realities to which atheistic Communists have pointed — will the true God begin to emerge as the ultimate reality within and beyond all realities, the God to whom human beings must respond. Any other idea of God, which tries to short-circuit the demands he makes on human creatures, is in effect atheism anyway. Thus Marxist atheism, taken seriously, can lead to the discovery of the living God, while thoughtless affirmations of Christian faith may in fact obscure his glory.

There is no denying that an engagement with atheism at this level is a tough debate, for which many Christians, with their comfortable notions of a Supreme Being governing human history with a special eye on the interests of Western civilization, are ill prepared. The temptation to which anti-Communism yields is that of attacking the crude anti-religious propaganda which forms the substance of campaigns in the Soviet Union and other Communist countries to indoctrinate citizens with so-called scientific atheism. Outdated, dull, and in fact thoroughly unscientific, this attack on religion runs as follows: At the beginning of human history, people lived in herds as equals. As time passed, the oldest and strongest came to exercise power over the others. The veneration of these elders was the beginning of religion. The idea of God as Lord of the universe is nothing more than a copy of these earthly powers at a somewhat higher level. He is the ruler of heaven, the ultimate slaveholder and judge, who has the power to punish or reward his subjects on earth. Faith in such a being is thus no more than a reflection of the abominable conditions in which most people live. And the church is an institution which deploys this faith to help the oppressors on earth to subdue the oppressed.

The cartoons illustrating this chapter make it evident how childish — and ultimately self-defeating — this anti-religious line can be. Atheist indoctrination thus exerts little influence over the minds of thousands of Communist-educated people, and Communism deceives itself when it considers such propaganda to be effective. Anti-Communist Christians are also on the wrong track when they seek to confront such arguments with an equally crude version of theistic faith. In trying to come to God's defense, they end up portraying him as a sort of old soldier who never dies, but simply fades away. Too often what they provide is material for further attacks on religion. Without the help of our weak but aggressive arguments, the God who showed himself as humble and defenseless at Bethlehem and again at Calvary discloses himself over and over to human beings, Christians and atheists alike. No one can escape *this* God, no matter how subtle the reasoning he or she employs.

Whether or not anti-Communists would admit it, there are elements other than the religious motive involved in anti-Communism. Psychological, economic, social, and cultural factors reinforce each other. To the anti-Communist, Communism is a monolithic whole, evil and threatening in every part. Thus a conspiracy psychology develops, a feeling that world events cannot be explained by ordinary processes but must reflect at every point the devious manipulations of the Enemy. Anti-Communism becomes an unconscious habit of mind: there need be no debate about it. In this uncritical form it colours many aspects of Western (particularly American) policy.

Seeing the world in black and white terms, the anti-Communist opposes not only Communism but also neutralism and democratic revolution. Fear of Communism becomes a camouflage for conservative and reactionary policies that seek to salvage as much of the status quo as can possibly be defended. Hand in hand with this goes a certainty that the Western world is incontrovertibly superior to the world of Communist countries and their satellites. The West is "the Free World," informed and nurtured by the Christian faith and dedicated to the preservation of Christian values. Committed to the principles of righteousness, justice, and peace, Western countries would never stoop to the practices of the Communists. Honesty and equity characterize all their dealings; and when they do go to war it is

Sign on the Russian Orthodox church building: "Landmark of 17th century: protected by the government." Sign over the entrance: "Detoxification station." Caption: "I won't go in! I am an atheist!"

always reluctantly and for the sake of bettering the lot of others.

The Western countries have given away billions of dollars to help the poor of the world. History will record that the United States has been the most philanthropic country ever. Multitudes of people have been fed with millions of tons of surplus foods, and technical aid has been bestowed on many nations. On this view, the only aim of all this beneficence is to lift the other peoples of the world to a higher standard of living and protect them from the theft of their liberties by Communists.

For all their passion, anti-Communists remain a mystery to much of the world. Underdeveloped nations, observing that the gap between themselves and the wealthy industrialized countries is widening not narrowing, do not share the sense that Communism is the primary menace to their attainment of a better life or that the American model is the surest route to it. To the anti-Communist, of course, such a response seems like sheer ingratitude. The rest of the world has been spoiled by Western benevolence.

It is important to emphasize that opposition to anti-Communism need not mean a denial of the basic incompatibility of Christianity and Marxism-Leninism. Quite the contrary. But what we have been suggesting is that equating Christianity with anti-Communism leads to a crude and over-simplified confrontation in which the real issues are totally obscured. Religious propaganda is, in its way, just as detrimental as anti-religious propaganda. When it is linked with that complex structure of ideas and ideals, beliefs and values, aspirations and standards, which some observers have called civil or civic religion — the synthesis of what is seen as the true, the good, and the right of Western civilization — religious propaganda becomes peculiarly powerful and dangerous. The "Western way of life" is not synonymous with the teachings of the Apostles' Creed; and zealous anti-Communists who confuse the two perform a great disservice.

Western civil religion — and in particular the American variety of it — does not prescribe what one should believe. It is a vague and all-purpose faith which may dissipate anxiety and guilt feelings and lead to personal self-acceptance but which also tends to be over-moralistic and to judge all problems as issues in which right and wrong can be clearly and simply distinguished. It was against the background of a similar "civil religion" in the Roman Empire that many early Christians were accused of atheism, because they refused to venerate the popular deities and worship the emperor.

Christians today must learn to see atheism as first of all a divine judgment on their own sins and failures. They should not shrink from admitting publicly that theism, including

Christian theism, has indeed been often used as an "opium for the masses." In the pointed words of the Russian philosopher Nicolas Berdyaev, "Communism is both the product of the godless West and at the same time the protest against godlessness."

Christians must be ready to cooperate with atheists in shaping the world we all must live in. To be sure, there must be a genuine encounter with atheism, but let no one think that dialogue may be confined to the doctrinal level. Above all, it is carried on in the testimony of life, both of individual Christians and of the whole church, a life of constant self-criticism and reform, a life in faith demonstrably free from comfortable superstitions and false security. Too often the need for that kind of encounter completely escapes the attention of those who enlist eagerly in the cause of "anti-Communism."

The Christian-Marxist Dialogue

Dialogue between Christians and Marxists, which began in the 1950s, flourished in the 1960s, as the East-West tensions of the Cold War relaxed somewhat. The de-Stalinization campaign in the Soviet Union, the tremendous changes in the Roman Catholic Church following the Second Vatican Council, and the growth of the ecumenical movement all contributed to bringing Christians and Marxists together for serious conversations about critical issues. A staggering output of literature on the subject appeared in English, French, German, Italian, and Spanish. Prominent participants from the Marxist side included Roger Garaudy, Milan Machovec, and Ernst Bloch; and such Christian theologians as Josef Hromadka, André Dumas, Karl Rahner, Harvey Cox, and James Luther Adams were involved at one time or another. After the Warsaw Pact forces, led by the Soviet Union, moved into Czechoslovakia in 1968 to cut short the liberalization movement led by Alexander Dubçek, the Christian-Marxist dialogue declined swiftly. Although it did not disappear entirely, encounters during the 1970s were less publicized and more widely diffused than earlier ones.

In the United States, Paul Mojzes continues to chair a task force on the Christian-Marxist Encounter of Christians

Associated for Relationships with Eastern Europe. A special winter 1978 issue of the *Journal of Ecumenical Studies*, of which Mojzes is managing editor, published 18 contributions on the dialogue between Marxists and Christians. In West Germany and Austria the Paulus-Gesellschaft, under the leadership of Erich Kellner, has resumed its sponsorship of symposia bringing together Marxist and Christian thinkers.

A variety of issues has been on the agendas for these encounters — atheism, transcendence, death, alienation, the individual and the community, Marxist and Christian eschatology, the search for the meaning of life, standards of morality. There is no doubt that the conversations have succeeded in eliminating some prejudices, misunderstandings, and false interpretations of each other's positions.

Marxists have openly admitted that religion is not always the "opium of the people," that Christianity in particular has sometimes been and can still be a protest against injustice and oppression and exploitation. They have conceded that socialism is by no means a magical leap from alienation to a de-alienated society. Since the contradictions of human

A Christian—Marxist dialogue sponsored by the WCC's sub-unit on Church and Society, Geneva, April 1968

WCC

social life cannot be erased by one grand act of liberation, Communists must constantly criticize dehumanizing tendencies in whatever form they arise and they must seek radical change as a ferment in even advanced socialist societies.

For their part, the Christians have pointed out that Marx and Feuerbach, in stressing that God is an idea of humanity, ignored the fact that God is a *necessary* idea, deeply rooted in all human beings. They have expressed their conviction that human efforts at social improvement can never make the gospel superfluous, and even in the most advanced and ideal Communist society there would be new questions that would not find answers from within the system. Only the Christian faith could provide an adequate response to such new disillusionments and perplexities. How far, they have asked, can Christians cooperate with Marxists without embracing Communism as the only true vision for human society?

Has this dialogue been useful? For many observers, especially among the young, Marxism is as "old hat" as the church. Christianity in the West betrays Christ by accommodating itself to the status quo, while the USSR betrays Marx by becoming just another bourgeois power. The dialogue between East and West is as antiquated and immaterial as the tension between the two. High-level academic discussions are unrelated to the political struggle for justice in a world which is divided not between Christians and Marxists but between the exploiters and the exploited.

Others have pointedly observed that the fundamental Marxist attitude toward Christianity has not changed because of these dialogues, the results of which have never really penetrated into the Communist Parties themselves. Faith in a personal God who reveals himself is still rejected as an antiquated superstition that depreciates human autonomy. Institutional churches must be classified as enemies of the Communist cause, and the attitude of government officials shows that the only real function of dialogue with individual Christians is to enlist as many of them as possible in the struggle for socialism. Churches in the East are tolerated if they proclaim their support for the upbuilding of the socialist state, but they are not considered an integral part of public social life.

The chief Marxist partners in the dialogue, almost all of whom have been expelled from Communist Parties, now tend toward a new utopian form of socialism. They view the problem of alienation as resulting not so much from private ownership and the exploitation of the proletariat by the bourgeoisie as from the oppressive and clumsy bureaucracy of the state system. Atheism is covered up by a new kind of Hegelian pantheism, but this is equally inimical to the Christian faith. In consequence these Marxists are not only marginal figures, but they are too antagonistic to each other to make significant dialogue with Christians possible.

Clearly the primary interest of Christians in continuing dialogue with Marxists should not be the mere fact of talking to Marxists, but the higher goal of enhancing human dignity, freedom, creativity, and wholeness. To the extent that Christian-Marxist dialogue misses the mark here, it must be modified or discontinued. What is needed is the increasing humanization of both Marxism and Christianity. There are some countries, particularly in Latin America, where the theoretical exchange of views in Christian-Marxist dialogue has attracted little interest. Instead, Christians and Communists have found themselves side by side in a common struggle against immediate and concrete cases of oppression and enforced dependency. These are situations in which Christianity and Marxism cannot be set over against each other as neat alternatives.

The revolution in Nicaragua in the fall of 1979 was a case of such cooperation. Many Christians gave thanks to God "for the victory of the Nicaraguan people, and for the instrument of freedom — the Sandinista Front of National Liberation." They had joined with other sectors of Nicaraguan society in the violent battle to overthrow the repressive and murderous Somoza regime. Five hundred evangelical pastors expressed their commitment to the new nation: "We commit ourselves to total cooperation with the works, projects, activities, and programs that the government may develop for the real benefit of the people." And they were explicit about the basis of that commitment: "This is with the understanding that our participation in any human project is related to our loyalty and faithfulness to the Lord Jesus Christ.''

In the neighbouring country of El Salvador, the Roman Catholic Archbishop Oscar Romero was murdered by the ultra-right to silence the outspoken positions he took on human rights, the oppression of the poor, and the systematic injustices committed against thousands of Salvadorean citizens. Confusion and terror at his funeral service led to many more deaths. Daily killings are the stock in trade of a military dictatorship which perpetuates itself in power in El Salvador — where two percent of the population owns sixty percent of the land. In such a society Christians and Marxists alike have only one choice: to work together for the overthrow of this oligarchy, which dominates farming and industry in close association with transnational corporations.

Sri Lanka is an example of a country in Asia where openness on the part of the Christian minority to several forces that shape social change, including Marxism and Buddhism, is required. Christians in Sri Lanka have formed new alliances. Collective farms have grown up, and relationships with the All Lanka Peasants' Congress have been developed. There is a network of core communities joined by the common goal of organizing and supporting peasant people in their struggle for a more just and human society.

Such examples of cooperation are not, of course, without their tensions. Marxists continue to challenge the bourgeois irresponsibility of many Christians; and Christians in turn raise pointed questions about the naive views of humanity, history, and God which many Marxists hold. Communists in such countries as Angola and Mozambique need to be shown that their understanding of revolution is simply not revolutionary enough. Their insights into the dynamics of social processes will fail if appropriated only to their own means and ends. No one suggests that Marxism should lead inevitably to Christianity. But by the same token, when Marxism is seen as the crucial determining element in the final synthesis, with Christianity to be used, subordinated, and finally cast aside, the idea of a pluralistic ''community

o our loyalty and faithfulness to the Lord

uring country of El Salvador, the Roman
shop Oscar Romero was murdered by the
nce the outspoken positions he took on
e oppression of the poor, and the systema-
mitted against thousands of Salvadorean
on and terror at his funeral service led to
s. Daily killings are the stock in trade of a
ip which perpetuates itself in power in El
two percent of the population owns sixty
nd. In such a society Christians and
only one choice: to work together for
his oligarchy, which dominates farming
e association with transnational corpo-

example of a country in Asia where
t of the Christian minority to several
cial change, including Marxism and
d. Christians in Sri Lanka have form
llective farms have grown up, and
All Lanka Peasants' Congress have
e is a network of core communities
goal of organizing and supporting
eir struggle for a more just and

peration are not, of course, without
continue to challenge the bourgeois
Christians; and Christians in turn
bout the naive views of humanity,
many Marxists hold. Communists
ola and Mozambique need to be
nding of revolution is simply not
eir insights into the dynamics of
f appropriated only to their own
uggests that Marxism should lead
But by the same token, when
cial determining element in the
ianity to be used, subordinated,
dea of a pluralistic "community

Associated for Relationships with Eastern Europe. A special winter 1978 issue of the *Journal of Ecumenical Studies*,
of which Mojzes is managing editor, published 18 contributions on the dialogue between Marxists and Christians. In
West Germany and Austria the Paulus-Gesellschaft, under
the leadership of Erich Kellner, has resumed its sponsorship
of symposia bringing together Marxist and Christian thinkers.

A variety of issues has been on the agendas for these
encounters — atheism, transcendence, death, alienation,
the individual and the community, Marxist and Christian
eschatology, the search for the meaning of life, standards of
morality. There is no doubt that the conversations have succeeded in eliminating some prejudices, misunderstandings,
and false interpretations of each other's positions.

Marxists have openly admitted that religion is not always
the "opium of the people," that Christianity in particular
has sometimes been and can still be a protest against injustice and oppression and exploitation. They have conceded
that socialism is by no means a magical leap from alienation
to a de-alienated society. Since the contradictions of human

A Christian—Marxist dialogue sponsored by the WCC's sub-unit on
Church and Society, Geneva, April 1968

WCC

social life cannot be erased by one grand act of liberation, Communists must constantly criticize dehumanizing tendencies in whatever form they arise and they must seek radical change as a ferment in even advanced socialist societies.

For their part, the Christians have pointed out that Marx and Feuerbach, in stressing that God is an idea of humanity, ignored the fact that God is a *necessary* idea, deeply rooted in all human beings. They have expressed their conviction that human efforts at social improvement can never make the gospel superfluous, and even in the most advanced and ideal Communist society there would be new questions that would not find answers from within the system. Only the Christian faith could provide an adequate response to such new disillusionments and perplexities. How far, they have asked, can Christians cooperate with Marxists without embracing Communism as the only true vision for human society?

Has this dialogue been useful? For many observers, especially among the young, Marxism is as "old hat" as the church. Christianity in the West betrays Christ by accommodating itself to the status quo, while the USSR betrays Marx by becoming just another bourgeois power. The dialogue between East and West is as antiquated and immaterial as the tension between the two. High-level academic discussions are unrelated to the political struggle for justice in a world which is divided not between Christians and Marxists but between the exploiters and the exploited.

Others have pointedly observed that the fundamental Marxist attitude toward Christianity has not changed because of these dialogues, the results of which have never really penetrated into the Communist Parties themselves. Faith in a personal God who reveals himself is still rejected as an antiquated superstition that depreciates human autonomy. Institutional churches must be classified as enemies of the Communist cause, and the attitude of government officials shows that the only real function of dialogue with individual Christians is to enlist as many of them as possible in the struggle for socialism. Churches in the East are tolerated if they proclaim their support for the upbuilding of the socialist state, but they are not considered an integral part of public social life.

The chief Marxist pa
whom have been expe
tend toward a new uto
problem of alienation
ownership and the e
bourgeoisie as from
of the state system.
of Hegelian panth
the Christian faith
only marginal fig
each other to m
possible.

Clearly the pr
dialogue with M
ing to Marxist
dignity, freed
that Christian
must be moc
increasing hu
There are s
where the
Marxist di
tians and
a commo
oppressi
in which
against

The
of suc
"for
stru
Libe
gua
an
pa
c
j

ject is related
Jesus Christ."
In the neighb
Catholic Archb
ultra-right to si
human rights, th
tic injustices con
citizens. Confusi
many more death
military dictatorsh
Salvador — where
percent of the la
Marxists alike hav
the overthrow of t
and industry in clo
rations.

Sri Lanka is an
openness on the pa
forces that shape s
Buddhism, is require
ed new alliances. C
relationships with the
been developed. Ther
joined by the commo
peasant people in th
human society.

Such examples of co
their tensions. Marxists
irresponsibility of many
raise pointed questions
history, and God which
in such countries as An
shown that their underst
revolutionary enough. T
social processes will fail
means and ends. No one s
inevitably to Christianity
Marxism is seen as the cr
final synthesis, with Christ
and finally cast aside, the i

of communities" has lost its meaning. The result is just one more totalitarianism.

Christians for Socialism

Before the middle of the nineteenth century — roughly contemporaneous with Karl Marx — "Christian socialism" had begun to emerge as a distinct movement. With its traditional affirmation that private property is inviolable, this early movement was not "socialistic" in the commonly accepted sense of the term, according to which private property is the root of all social ills.

The first leaders of Christian socialism in England were F. D. Maurice (1805-1872) and Charles Kingsley (1819-1875). Their programme included the call for cooperative workshops and distributive societies, the passage of social legislation, and the availability of improved education. In Germany Archbishop Wilhelm E. von Ketteler (1811-1877) of Mainz was instrumental in founding continental Catholic socialism. He argued that the one true solution to social problems was the "principle of association," which called for the formation of Christian cooperative bodies. In France Charles Forbes René de Montalembert (1810-1870) urged reforms in the interest of the working class, including social insurance and wage-and-hour legislation, and the adoption of democracy, while opposing state socialism.

A parallel movement in the United States, with some fallout in Europe as well, was the Social Gospel movement associated with the name of the American Baptist minister Walter Rauschenbusch (1861-1918). The familiar slogan "the fatherhood of God and the brotherhood of men" summed up the model of society for which the Social Gospel appealed. People were considered to be essentially good and thus open and responsive to moral persuasion; sin was seen as primarily selfishness. The movement was by no means unaware that sin is transmitted corporately through corrupt human institutions, but it believed that social salvation would come as individuals and institutions were brought under the law of love.

The influence of the Social Gospel movement was strengthened through the Federal Council of the Churches of

Christ in the USA (later the National Council of Churches), which was founded in 1908 at the height of the movement. It waned between the world wars with the rise of a less optimistic theological mood, fueled by the turbulence and political catastrophes ravaging European civilization. But even today evidences of it remain among Christians working to better society, in their strong emphasis on political activism and their passionate concern for justice. Conversely, contemporary opponents of this sort of active Christian involvement in society are quick to use the term "Social Gospel" to discredit such programmes.

Among the great Christian theologians of the previous generation, two should be singled out for their socialist outlook, Paul Tillich (1886-1965) and Karl Barth (1886-1968). Tillich believed that socialism was essentially in harmony with the Christian outlook, though it needed to be corrected and enriched. He wrote in *The Protestant Era* that "religious socialism energetically carries on the cultural criticism characteristic of all socialism and seeks to lead the latter to its own real depth." As a leader of the German church struggle from 1933-1945, Barth upset many of his Christian contemporaries by declaring that National Socialism was a far more insidious threat than Soviet Communism.

The 1968 assembly of the Roman Catholic bishops of Latin America at Medellin, Colombia proved to be a watershed in the church's involvement in the social struggle in that part of the world. Since then, many Latin American church leaders have become increasingly explicit in their critique of the capitalist system and of the "international imperialism of money." Among the most significant groups to be formed was the Christians for Socialism movement, focused in Chile at the beginning, but quickly suppressed by the Chilean junta after its first conference in Santiago in April 1972. The movement spread quickly in Latin America, however, then to North America and Europe. An international meeting took place in Quebec in April 1975, and the European group met in Milan in May 1979, under the co-sponsorship of the World Student Christian Federation.

The approach of Christians for Socialism differs considerably from that of their counterparts in previous generations. They speak openly of capitalist imperialism and of the need to join the class struggles in the world on the side of the oppressed masses. Rather than setting up their own groups, Christians for Socialism join existing class-oriented organizations of workers and peasants. The specific Christian contribution to socialism, they believe, is not something that Christians bring ready-made to the revolutionary struggle, but something that emerges in the life-experience of that struggle as the Christian faith reveals previously unsuspected creative resources.

According to Christians for Socialism, the unequal and contradictory character of the worldwide expansion of capitalist imperialism has become obvious in our time. Capital and technology are more and more concentrated in the hands of multinational and transnational firms based in North America and Europe. With government support they invade the entire world through their subsidiaries. If democratic or authoritarian regimes cannot guarantee them the high rate of profit and the security they desire, they do not hesitate to transfer their activities to countries where they can be protected by totalitarian governments who brutally suppress trade unions and political activities. Thus the international struggle has assumed a new form; the multinational companies, allied with the bourgeoisie of the countries where they operate, are the most powerful enemy.

Christians for Socialism want to purify the church and sever the links between Christianity and those who hold economic and political power in this way. They point out that most Christians in the wealthy countries have no idea how their brothers and sisters elsewhere in the world are being exploited. The seeds of a popular church must be sown, and Christians who have spiritualized the faith must be made conscious that the proclamation of the Word and the celebration of the Eucharist are symbols of faithfulness to Christ only when they are also recognized as pointing to his liberating struggle on the side of the poor.

A "materialistic" interpretation of the Bible has arisen in connection with these emphases of Christians for Socialism. On this view, the life of Jesus must be related directly to the "class struggle" as it existed in his day. His suffering and dying were *political* events liberating humanity from poverty, oppression, sin, and ignorance. Jesus did not preach submission and resignation; he condemned the exploiting rich. Matthew's gospel records him as saying that he had come to bring not peace but a sword. His own crucifixion identified him with the slaves, fugitives, outcasts, and political insurgents; and he told his followers to take up their cross and follow him. Tragically, however, the church ignored or forgot that the cross was an instrument of torture inflicted by the ruling class on slaves, and cross-bearing came to be spiritualized as an act of penance and self-denial.

According to materialist interpretation of Scripture, much of the New Testament cannot be explained apart from an understanding of concrete social and political data. The reader must not ignore the impact of modes of production, class struggle, and the relationship of religious loyalties to political powers. A genuine Christian theology, one which begins with the difficulties and risks of the daily social struggles of the underprivileged classes, will decipher the meaning of political and ideological battles in the light of Christ's struggle against the enslaving principalities and powers.

Critics of Christians for Socialism and materialist exegesis counter that the Bible is rooted in its own historical situation, with all of its own dangers, problems, and challenges. Those who ignore this turn the Scriptures into a myth and theology into mere metaphysics. The overwhelming danger of any talk about a "fruitful dialectic between social practice and divine revelation" or about the "dynamic between militancy and faith" is that God's disclosure of himself in his Son will thereby be used to sanction one's previous ideological commitment. And who has the right to prescribe the correct political choice or the norm of firm and appropriate action?

If the Bible is to be read as a witness to the class struggle and to Jesus' total involvement in it, one must in effect establish a new canon of Scripture within the canon accepted by the church from the beginning. And, the critics of materialist exegesis conclude, Christians for Socialism have been unable to succeed in such a dubious exercise. They have built their biblical theology on the sand of the Marxist analysis of society. But (to change the image) one cannot pick and choose from Marxism as if it were a grocery store; and if Christians for Socialism begin to shop there, they will eventually buy everything. However important an understanding of the process of class struggle may be to the reader of Scripture, it simply cannot explain everything.

There is no doubt that some significant insights have emerged out of this debate over the last decade. But the fundamental questions remain unanswered: on what basis is a Christian partisan politics to be founded and how is it to be applied to complex social and political situations? Merely saying that Christians can gain life-experience in the revolutionary struggle and thus provide creative contributions to it bypasses the critical problem of spelling out the theoretical and practical differences between socialism and Communism. Christians who adopt a partisan socialist position are obliged to clarify how far the social and economic aspects of peoples' lives can be engineered without destroying the very elements that make people human. They must take seriously the fact that individual self-interest and the collective selfishness of nations always corrupt efforts for human liberation and economic justice.

Another difficulty Christians for Socialism face is the choice of direction in their social and political battles. Some of them believe that the ideological struggle against the churches' betrayal of the poor and oppressed must be led from the outside and aim at exposing the apathy and irrelevance of Christian institutions. Others argue that the struggle must come from within, "conscientizing" as many Christians within the churches as possible. Still others contend that whatever action is taken must lead to a renewal of the Christian faith and perhaps develop new community structures as a result.

The ambiguous and incomplete address of Christians for Socialism to problems like these reflects its lack of inner unity and prevents it from growing into a viable international movement.

IV. The ecumenical movement

Critics of the ecumenical movement, particularly in Europe and North America, have accused the World Council of Churches of exchanging the vision of unity which brought it into being for an all-out identification with revolutionary Marxist theory and strategy. Prominent among outspoken WCC opponents in recent years are Edward Norman, a lecturer in history at Cambridge, and Ernest W. Lefever, a lecturer in government at Georgetown University in Washington, D.C., and founding director of the Ethics and Public Policy Center.* Their extended attacks on programmes undertaken by the WCC have been picked up by numerous religious and secular journalists; and they have been influential as well among members of churches affiliated with the WCC and Christian groups outside of its fellowship.

The WCC has, according to this interpretation, an unhealthy obsession with the problems of the Third World. The ecumenical leadership suffers from the illusion that quick reform and rapid transformation of unjust and underdeveloped societies is within the realm of possibility. Its naive and stereotyped view of the Third World gravely underestimates the fragility and pauperism of the many nations in Asia, Africa, and Latin America which are run by authoritarian élites. The range of political and economic choices open to such countries is very narrow. Yet their envy of the power and wealth of the West gives birth to great expectations. Communist-inspired shortcuts to order, modernization, and affluence only to lead to more misery, insecurity, and dependence.

Activist ecumenical Christians, their common sense swept away by the moral fervour of their convictions, are — like all leftist movements — unaware of how swiftly an ideal promoted for one reason can give way to other, less noble motivations. To identify Christ with passing human enthusiasm

---

* Norman's Reith Lectures, sponsored by the BBC, were subsequently published by Oxford University Press under the title *Christianity and the World Order* (1979); the same year saw the publication by Georgetown University of Lefever's *Amsterdam to Nairobi: The World Council of Churches and the Third World*.

is to lose him amidst the shifting superstructure of human idealism. The Marxist understanding of how the historical process works cannot be accepted without traditional Christian correctives.

Lefever argues that Christian communities are not, cannot be, and thus should not represent themselves as competent in complex economic and political issues. The expertise of the church is ethical judgment. In the name of all that Christianity stands for, churches should speak out tirelessly against genocide, against the refusal of governments to permit impartial humanitarian aid to civilian victims of war and natural disaster, against any case of gross inhumanity. The wise and morally responsible course for Christians is to encourage peaceful and lawful forces which are trying to deal constructively with poverty, racism, and injustice. Above all, the right to judge any political movement or system by universal Christian standards must be maintained.

Other commentators have stressed that the most important thing for Christianity to rediscover today is a profound sense of historical relativism. In the high-stakes game of international politics, manipulated by ruthless Communist forces, there is a moral obligation to be firm, shrewd, and intelligent. Christian leftists, by contrast, demonstrate none of these qualities. They misconceive reality in demonstrable ways. Liberation theology, so highly esteemed in many quarters, utterly lacks a scientific sociological basis; and the failure of the ecumenical leadership to realize this only makes the shrill voices of anti-capitalism ever more strident.

In the scope of a short book like this one we cannot undertake a point-by-point rebuttal of the various forms — some detailed and thoughtful, others rhetorical and caricatured — which this critique has assumed in recent years. Instead, taking a closer look at three areas on the agenda of the WCC, we shall try to demonstrate how such divisive issues have inevitably arisen as the churches seek to move together toward visible unity, particularly since the WCC's inaugural assembly at Amsterdam in 1948. We shall look first at the work of the Faith and Order Commission, next at the controversial Programme to Combat Racism, and finally at the recent emphasis on a "just, participatory, and sustainable society."

Faith and Order

The Faith and Order movement — whose history antedates that of the WCC, of which it is now a Commission — has been a key instrument over the years in helping churches to reflect on what it means to belong to the one Body of Christ and how we are to understand the visible manifestations of this. For over fifty years it has focused on the doctrinal and theological issues which divide Christianity. Significant worldwide agreement has emerged on some of these issues, particularly in the recent Faith and Order projects "Giving Account of the Hope That Is In Us" and "Towards an Ecumenical Consensus on Baptism, Eucharist, and Ministry."

But it has slowly dawned on Christian communities that unity is not just a matter of agreeing on common theological statements and working toward common ecclesiastical practices. Beyond the unity of the church, the unity of the whole human race is at stake. Recognizing this, in the early 1970s Faith and Order launched a study of "the unity of the church and the unity of humankind." Although some have protested that this theme is a betrayal of the real task of the ecumenical movement, others argue that this study project has not moved far enough beyond its initial stage. Many Christians are convinced that the examination of how concrete human issues, one by one, bear on the question of church unity will disclose that what is central today is not the traditional denominational and confessional fragmentation but still deeper human divisions that invade and divide the church as well. How does the contemporary human situation relate to the claims of the church and its faith?

The Commission on Faith and Order has made progress in bringing specific problems of human division into a context where church unity is the central interest. Its work on "Racism in Theology, Theology Against Racism," its effort to discover the wholeness of the family of God in and with disabled persons, and its study of the community of women and men in the church are three recent cases of what have been called "inter-contextual" studies relating broader problems of human disunity to the search for unity in the church. Already in 1952, at the third World Conference on Faith and Order (Lund, Sweden), the bearing of "non-theological" elements on Christian unity was acknowledged. But because of the lip-service paid to these factors, it was not until recently that the importance of geo-political, social, racial, and cultural considerations has emerged with full seriousness. These will form an important part of the theological work of the 1980s.

Clearly, more and deeper inter-contextual and interdisciplinary studies of the how and why of Christian communion in the world are called for. How can churches which practice intercommunion and even become structurally united claim to be one in Christ when all sorts of discrimination and segregation flourish in their congregations? What kind of unity is it which allows the enrichment of one sector of the church at the expense of others? What kind of community permits women and disabled persons to remain on the fringes?

At a rally in Lausanne on Pentecost 1977, celebrating the anniversary of the first World Conference on Faith and Order held in the same city fifty years earlier, WCC General Secretary Philip Potter spoke these words of challenge to the ecumenical movement:

> The unity of the church is not an ecclesiastically domestic affair. It concerns the whole human race. Just as the divisions and conflicts of the churches are signs and reflections of the divisions in our world, so the unity of the church is a sign and sacrament of God's purpose to unite all into Christ as the head of a new humanity and a new creation. We are called to work for overcoming the barriers which exist between human beings — barriers of race, of sex, of wealth and poverty, of political conflict.

Those who respond to such a visionary appeal must keep a sharp eye out for lofty abstractions and triumphalist ecumenical phrase-making. For there are other movements and people — Marxists prominent among them — who also claim to be working to overcome the barriers to the spiritual harmony and physical well-being of the human community. What movement, what group, can be trusted, listened to, and followed? What community offers the greatest insight, on the basis of the widest experience, in struggling against the wrongs of human society?

That is why there is more to the question of the unity of the church than preoccupation with the racism, the fate of disabled persons, and the discrimination against women in its own ranks — as undeniably important as these are. Only if the churches face human discontinuity and conflict ever more openly can they discover and communicate God's continuity and reconciliation in history. During its meeting in August 1980 the Central Committee of the WCC struggled with the theme "The Church *of* the Poor." There had been plenty of talk during the preceding decade about the church *for* the poor, and the church *in solidarity with* the poor. Many of the world's marginal and starving people, particularly in Asia, live entirely outside of the church's fellowship. The question must be raised as to whether the concept of the church *of* the poor will lead to an enlargement of the eucharistic communion of many of the privileged of the world.

The ecumenical movement, particularly through the efforts of Faith and Order, has taught us a great deal about Christian unity as the gathering of God's people through one baptism, in one eucharist, and by one ministry. But Christian unity must equally be seen as identification with Christ in his cry of separation from God and as participation in the reconciling power of his risen life. If this humble task of reconciliation does not take place in the midst of the strife between those who offer conflicting blueprints for human society, the unity of the church will tragically be no more than an "ecclesiastically domestic affair." Christians will withdraw conveniently into their ghettos.

Make no mistake about it: it is no easy task to overcome "barriers of race, of sex, of wealth and poverty, of political conflict" — and to do so more effectively than others who offer their own models for society. Just how difficult it can be will emerge as we take a closer look at the WCC's Programme to Combat Racism. In so doing we will confront policy issues that bear on other WCC programmes as well.

The Struggle against Racism

Like other Christian bodies, the World Council of Churches has often condemned racism, issuing various strong statements against it. In 1969 its Programme to Combat Racism was initiated, and soon two new tactics were deployed in the struggle. First, churches were challenged to discontinue their economic support (in the form of investments) for South Africa, whose official government policies stamped it as the epitome of white racism. Many churches responded positively to this appeal. Second, the PCR offered churches a way to identify in some small degree with racially oppressed groups by setting up a Special Fund. To date, this Fund has transferred about $3.5 million to such groups and movements. Beyond the condition that the money be used for humanitarian or educational purposes, the PCR Special Fund exercises no control over the use of these grants.

Behind these two new tactics in the church's ongoing opposition to racism lay several convictions. First is the judgment that white racism, supported by long-standing and powerful structures in society, is by far the most dangerous element in present racial conflicts. Moreover, the struggle against racism must not be limited to attacking the prejudices of individuals, but must take account of social, political, and economic structures which institutionalize racial oppression. The battle against racism must entail a redistribution of political, economic, and cultural power; and no single strategy will be universally appropriate for this. Belief in the inherent superiority of a particular race and its right to dominate others must be challenged on every front. Finally, the question of racial conflicts has become increasingly international: no longer is it possible for a government to claim that its racial problems are its own purely domestic concern.

The PCR has been subject to frequent criticism, much of it based on misrepresentations of what it has attempted and undertaken. (Ironically, understanding of its aims and support for it have increased at the same time.) The most common charge leveled against the PCR Special Fund is that the money it makes available for humanitarian and educational

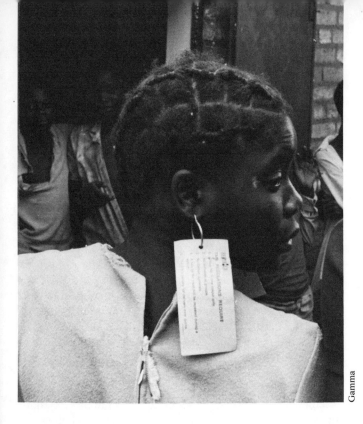

purposes either frees other funds or is itself diverted for military purposes, so that money given by Christian churches ends up supporting violent and subversive actions which Christians cannot endorse. Later in this section we shall look more closely at the question of Christianity and violence.

The strongest protest came as a result of two grants in the latter part of 1978. These were made, in the words of Ernest W. Lefever, "to Marxist-led guerrilla groups: $85,000 to the so-called Patriotic Front, which was seeking to shoot its way into power in Rhodesia, and $125,000 to SWAPO, which was fighting toward the same objective in South West Africa — both against interim interracial regimes."

Contrary to Lefever's analysis, the Patriotic Front of Joshua Nkomo and Robert Mugabe did not "shoot its way into power" in Zimbabwe-Rhodesia. At the new constitutional conference in London in September 1979, the Patriotic Front was recognized as a full and legitimate partner in the discussions; and it signed, along with the other partners, the Lancaster House agreement, which paved the way for free elections. In those elections Mugabe, who became Prime Minister, gained 57 of the 80 black representatives in parliament, while Bishop Abel Muzorewa, who had called for a "democratic and constitutional" approach to change, secured only three seats.

Zimbabwe still faces innumerable problems of reconstruction. Refugees must be resettled, the economic system overhauled, mass education and health care made available. But under the circumstances the elections produced the best possible solution in terms of peace and stability. The armed struggle was given the stamp of overwhelming popular approval, and the leaders of the new government are committed to building up a nonracial society. Of course every situation is unique, and Christians discredit their own pretensions to special insights into social and economic realities when they allow themselves to be blinded to the particularities of a situation by their partisan biases — whether liberal or conservative. But it would be self-righteous and disastrous if the churches would capitulate to Lefever's claim that "the condition of the Third World cannot be changed, but must be faced and endured."

Too often those who accuse the WCC of naive support for Marxist liberation movements either do not understand or else refuse to admit the intimate connection between the demand for growth in the Gross National Product of the rich nations and the need for rebellion by those peoples who are starving, diseased, and ignorant. When the call for "ecumenical moderation instead of ecumenical radicalism" means ignoring the link between the fate of the rich and the fate of the poor, it is a deceptive and unevangelical appeal.

The demand for a rejection of violence, frequently heard in this context, can cloud the issue further. Forces which appear to be "law-abiding" and "peaceful" may be covertly more violent in fact than those who take up arms to overthrow them. It should be clear that violence is not necessarily to be equated with radicalism and revolution, nor nonviolence with gradualism and reform. It should be even clearer that Jesus' proclamation of the kingdom of God reveals a much deeper reality: that the perpetuation of the circle of violence and counter-violence is broken by his power as Saviour.

The intricate issue of violence and nonviolence is at the heart of all social life, particularly in the realm of relationships between the races. White Christians must be especially wary of using the term "nonviolence," because it can so easily be a code word for maintaining an oppressive status quo. The power of the crucified Christ can help us grasp in greater depth that racist human beings — and that includes everyone — create racist structures of society and that those racist structures in turn confirm and reinforce individual racist attitudes. The demonic pervasiveness of racism compels Christians to speak of collective sin. All people are thrown together in the solidarity of hate and prejudice. No one is free self-righteously to dissociate himself or herself from these evils. The only way out of the web of our inhumanity to each other is to take the risk of making ourselves vulnerable.

Conscious of the depth of human sin and the fierceness of the struggle with the "principalities and powers" that lie behind racial oppression, committed Christians recognize the need for transferring political and economic might from the powerful to the powerless. As ambassadors of Christ's reconciliation, informed by the gospel, they are under no illusions that sin is the exclusive property of one group of people or the other. Consequently, efforts such as the PCR will inevitably confront tangled situations in which involvement will not be without its risks. From the false security of the sidelines there will come charges of uncritical acceptance of Marxist goals and strategies and betrayal of the mission of the church.

Such accusations must be firmly rejected. The church which shrinks back from sharing meaningfully in Christ's own anger over the destructiveness of racial sin has forfeited its calling to "let justice roll down like waters and righteousness like an ever-flowing stream" (Amos 5:24). Above the clamor of its critics, the church must make its voice against racism and racist structures, East and West, North and South, heard ever louder, ever clearer.

A Just, Participatory and Sustainable Society

We have seen in this chapter how the ecumenical concern for Christian unity has inevitably broadened to recognize the need for an engagement with the divisive issues that affect all of humanity. In the church's response to racism, one of the most persistent and dangerous of these factors, we saw a specific example of how Christians cannot avoid the risks of involvement in an arena where others, Marxists included, have made competing claims to offer authentic and workable solutions. There is no way for ecumenical theology to divorce itself from politics. The remainder of this chapter will be devoted to examining the effort by the World Council of Churches in the last several years to address divisive social issues more systematically through its programme emphasis on a "just, participatory, and sustainable society."

The concept of a "sustainable and just society" was introduced in the report of a 1974 conference in Bucharest on the Future of Man and Society in a World of Science-Based Technology. The report foresaw "a world where (1) the security of the individual, (2) the redistribution of material wealth, and (3) the implementation of a maximum consumption level are affected by a transnational social security system dividing the responsibility for the fate of the individual among all people." This idea was debated during the 1975 assembly of the WCC in Nairobi, and in 1977 the Central Committee mandated an advisory group to stimulate further theological and ethical reflection on it.

Several elements were singled out for attention at that time:

— What Christian theological and ethical insights shape the idea of a just, participatory, and sustainable society?

— Some Christians involved in the struggle for a better society have called for "Christian realism" in combatting the influence of sin in the world; others have offered a more idealistic vision, which has sometimes been called "utopian." How do the resources of Christian theology bear on each of these approaches?

— Recent Christian thinkers have used the New Testament language about "principalities and powers" (for example, in Romans 8:38 and Colossians 2:15) to illuminate the nature of the struggle for social improvement. How is this first-century idea to be understood today?

— In the widespread contemporary concern with ecology and the use of the earth's finite resources, Christianity often gets the blame for a wasteful and exploitative attitude which has contributed to worsening environmental problems. How do Christian perspectives on creation, nature, and history relate to this issue?

— What do Christians have to say about science and technology and their consequences for the quality of life on earth?

— How should Christians see the role of dialogue with persons of other faiths and ideologies in the struggle for a new global society?

The focal point of this new ecumenical programme theme is *justice*. The two other elements, participation and sustainability, are necessary dimensions of the contemporary struggle for justice. From the point of view of the kingdom of God, justice is not a principle or an ideal value which will never be fully realized. Rather, as the historical embodiment of love, it indicates a quality of relationships in community and a criterion for evaluating and changing social structures.

The biblical reality at the root of the idea of *participation* is fellowship (*koinonia*). Christians can and must work together in the realization that their faith is not a mere private affair between the individual and God. But how can participation be organized and guaranteed? How can people be freed from being at the mercy of the "experts" and given greater control over the direction of developments in science and technology? How can human relationships and community be maintained in the struggle against impersonal structures of nationalism and internationalism?

The concept of *sustainability* brings to the fore the critical problem that the achievement of a high level of consumption in developed countries is in many ways the result of their exploitation of the rest of the world. A further dilemma is raised by the need to attain material growth that is ecologically sustainable. Can an acceptable life be achieved in the short run while avoiding long-term setbacks? Will permanent global solidarity require a drastic elimination of differentials in income, wealth, and power in the industrialized countries? Does economic development in less industrialized nations, if it is to be sustainable, first require a redistribution of wealth?

The issues surrounding the "just, participatory, and sustainable society" are obviously fundamental ones, calling for both Christian action and Christian thought. Member churches must be drawn into active sharing in this programme, seeking to understand themselves better and helping each other towards renewal. But there are also items here for the agenda of Christian thinkers, who must undertake their theological and ethical reflection in full awareness of the desperate struggles and complicated international situations which affect the lives of most of the world's population. One of these issues is the question of violence and nonviolence — a far more complex problem, as we saw in the preceding section, than many Christians are willing to admit. The problem of power, too, demands critical and informed Christian thought. The sinful dimension of power, which perverts human relationships and contradicts basic human aspirations, is one side of this issue; but we must also rediscover the messianic and liberating power of Jesus Christ and the challenges it can pose to debased structures of political, economic, military, and scientific-technological power.

Let us conclude this look at the programme emphasis on a "just, participatory, and sustainable society" by mentioning briefly the ongoing response to it in two departments of the WCC. The sub-unit on Dialogue with People of Living Faiths and Ideologies has emphasized, as its name suggests, the common search for community in all the world. People of various faiths and ideologies are caught up together in social, economic, political, and environmental interdependence. They cannot escape the challenge of seeking new patterns of community in which others can participate fully. This concern is not an exclusively Christian prerogative. The common quest for a more meaningful and sustaining community raises questions about the resources of all living faiths and ideologies for undergirding personal and communal values.

The "Guidelines on Dialogue," issued by this sub-unit in 1979 after lengthy discussions, focus more on religious dialogue than on the encounter between Christianity and ideologies, largely because there has been more experience of dialogue with people of living faiths. But there is general agreement that further work in the area of dialogue with ideologies is necessary. The "external dialogue" with persons of living ideologies will succeed only if there is first a process of "internal dialogue" about the ideological dimensions of religion and the religious dimensions of ideologies.

The Commission on the Churches' Participation in Development (CCPD) has found its own specific entree into the debate on a "just, participatory, and sustainable society." After ten years of exploration and evaluation it is now able to speak more articulately of "the church of the poor." In 1975 the Nairobi assembly spoke of understanding development "as a liberating process aimed at justice, self-reliance and economic growth. It is essentially a people's struggle, in which the poor and the oppressed are and should be the active agents and immediate beneficiaries. Seen in this perspective the role of the churches and the World Council of Churches is to support the struggle of the poor and the oppressed towards justice and self-reliance."

Now it is added that Christian solidarity with the poor and the exploited is only real if development is not *for* the poor, but can be achieved *by* them and *with* them as they become full participants in the processes which lead to justice and liberation. Everything hinges on the organized struggle of the poor, which indicates an awareness of their own social power. People's organization is the link between goals and action, theory and practice, the dynamic element which preserves the relation between what people want to achieve and how, when, and where to progress towards such goals.

Christianity can no longer afford to hand the poor a ready-made theology. Poor people struggling for justice read the Bible and find that it comes alive in new ways as the liberation to which it witnesses is seen as liberation in

action. The Scriptures do not deal with situations of despe-
ration and want in abstract terms. Their interest is less in
"the problem of poverty" than in the poor themselves and
in the oppressive acts of those who make and keep them
poor. Not that the Bible idealizes or romanticizes the poor;
but because God is on their side they provide a motive for
the manifestation of his justice and love. The millions of
poor people are not something out there to which the church
relates, but an integral and structuring part of the whole
community of faith. Because Christ utterly identifies himself with the oppressed, the destitute, and the abandoned,
he is the permanent disturber of the organization, teaching,
and liturgy of the church whenever these become factors of
oppression and alienation.

All this talk of a "just, participatory, and sustainable
society" can of course become nothing more than hifalutin
ecumenical jargon, a bell that we can hear tolling but cannot
say where. The need is for concrete actions. This programme of the WCC and its member churches will not get
off the ground if it does not inspire what we shall be calling
in the last chapter "people-politics." Justice, full participation, and sustainability require tireless efforts undertaken
on the basis of unambiguous convictions.

V. Christians and political involvement

The member churches of the World Council of Churches live and work in a variety of social and political situations. Individual Christians in these denominations face widely diverse challenges as they seek to work out the implications of their faith in their own particular contexts. Given these differences, it would be out of the question for the WCC or any organization like it to specify responsible political choices for those who want to share in the vision of a "just, participatory, and sustainable society," outlined briefly in the preceding chapter. To put it in the terms of this book, "a Christian *can* be a socialist, but a Christian is not *bound* to be a socialist," as the German theologian Hans Küng observes in *On Being a Christian*.

Consider some of the contexts in which Christians today live. It would make no sense to replace the social democratic system of the Netherlands with a Maoist-oriented political ideology. Sri Lanka would jeopardize the entire fabric of its society and create even more exploitation and injustice if it were to adopt an economic pattern of free enterprise and an uncontrolled market. The much-heralded model of African socialism being tried in Tanzania is still out of reach for many other African countries because of their own historical background and current developments. Christians in France do not necessarily need to join hands with the Communists as some of their desperate fellow Christians have seen the need to do in El Salvador. What choice do Filipino Christians have but to close ranks with Muslims against the abuses of martial law by President Marcos? What option does the church in Burma have but to contribute with Buddhists to finding socialist solutions for national problems?

Similar awareness of particular contextual factors is necessary with respect to public reaction by the WCC to events in Eastern Europe. Trumpeting WCC criticism of an Eastern European government in the Western press — as some Council critics have called for — is offensive, ineffective, even counter-productive. Those who head up the religious affairs departments in these socialist states will listen and eventually react only if complaints and pleas for change are addressed directly to them. Eastern churches have warned their Western brothers and sisters not to draw exclusive attention to the lot of dissidents. Surely Christians and other disaffected persons who are imprisoned or confined in psychiatric hospitals by Communist regimes need support from the West. But singling them out as the exemplary martyrs of our day only marginalizes even more the established Christian communions there. Defending human rights in a liberal Western fashion can play directly into the hands of the Communists, offering them a welcome alibi for reducing further the religious freedom allowed to millions of the faithful.

Whatever political options Christians face in their own contexts, the overriding fact remains that the "haves" of this world lord it over the "have nots"; and there are no signs that the powerful and affluent intend to give up their competition for economic and military dominion or renounce their imperialism against smaller countries in their sphere of influence and Third World nations. At the same time, serious work on finding solutions for the energy crisis, the depletion of world resources, and the pollution of the environment has not yet started on either the capitalist or the Communist side. Most countries in the First and Second World export great quantities of weapons to any nation interested in buying them for whatever purpose. All of the political parties in France, for example, from the ultra-right to the ultra-left, make no objection to the sale of sophisticated weapons to South Africa. French labour unions are primarily interested in keeping employment high and raising their members' living standards. The lucrative production and sale of arms by Switzerland is sanctioned by the majority of the Swiss on the ground that additional millions are needed to defend its own legendary neutrality.

Such factors bear decisively on political attitudes at the local level. How many American citizens realize that the economic boom in Brazil (if they are aware of it at all) benefits very few Brazilians, most of whom live at or below the poverty line; or that it is largely conditioned by American investment policy and protected by the watchful eye of the Central Intelligence Agency over the military junta? Similar issues are raised by American involvement in economic, political, and military affairs elsewhere in Latin America.

Nor should their indignation over the Soviet invasion of Afghanistan lead Americans to forget the long and destructive US intervention in Vietnam, supporting a corrupt regime and in the process dropping more bombs on a small country than fell on Europe during all of World War II.

Western Christians, when they are politically oriented, tend to concentrate unduly on domestic issues. To be sure, the list of nagging internal problems that plague a country like the United States is long and daunting. The middle classes are hurt by inequalities in the tax system, inflation, unemployment, rising costs for health care and higher education. In the cities, three groups of people face a grim and uncertain future. Unskilled or semi-skilled labourers, who do not own their homes and cannot get enough support from government, from stable families, or from effective unions, feel increased pressure, particularly during periods of economic slowdown. Unemployed minority youth threaten to become a permanent underclass with no means to bring about change on their own initiative. Elderly persons struggling to meet essential needs with moderate fixed incomes are offered woefully inadequate medical and housing programmes, and they become more and more marginalized in a society obsessed with the economic clout of people between 18 and 35.

The military-industrial complex — despite warnings twenty years ago from President Eisenhower, himself one of the most-respected American military leaders of this century — assumes an ever-greater role in determining social and economic planning. Centralized government and unresponsive bureaucracies dominate more and more of human life. In the face of this state power, the cherished American ideal of pluralism has not promoted the dispersal of economic power, and too often rhetoric about the pluralist ideal serves as a façade behind which a few control everything through an artificial market mechanism.

Where do the churches operate in this system? Christian denominations and agencies have demonstrated a notable capacity to sponsor conferences and programmes for "raising the consciousness" of their members, even to explore and test alternative models of social organization and life-style. They have become aware of a level in society in which a fabric of solidarity, mutual support, and trust can be built. But it remains an open question whether intentional actions by the churches and their agencies at this level of society, which sociologists have called the "mezzo-structure," can meaningfully address the superstructure or substructure.

What is needed is critical and systematic analysis of how the so-called free-market system operates and how it assumes so decisive a role in the economic and political development of the world. Such painstaking analysis really depends on collective government initiative and parliamentary decision, and these are in the realm of the superstructure. Too often the approach of Christian churches to global corporations, domestic political parties, and educational and service institutions is piecemeal and scattershot, bypassing the problems of blatant social and economic justice both at home and abroad.

Our emphasis in the last few paragraphs has been on the situation of Christians in America. But there are parallels in other Western countries as well. The United Nations has proposed that a standard figure for development aid by a wealthy nation ought to be seven-tenths of one percent of that country's Gross National Product. Only Norway, Sweden, and the Netherlands meet that minimal figure (interestingly, these are also the only three governments to contribute directly to the Special Fund of the WCC's Programme to Combat Racism). One can argue, of course, that these are small nations which face far fewer domestic poverty problems than lands such as the USA.

All this does not contradict the remark of Hans Küng cited earlier. It does not add up to the conclusion that Christians must become adherents of doctrinaire socialism and advocate collective government ownership and administration of the means of production and control of the distribution of goods. On the other hand, Christian communities in the West surely need to do a better job of recognizing their tacit identification with national structures of society, especially to the extent that these are based on anachronistic ideas about the vigorous individual pursuit of happiness and security. The glib affirmation that "I lead a decent life and meet the standards of goodness" is a façade of selfishness and ignorance. Casual acceptance of the status quo often leads to a fear of or aversion to any movement for social change, particularly once such an initiative is labeled "socialistic."

Very different national problems and political issues confront churches and Christians in the Second World, where the whole of society is increasingly permeated by Marxist ideology. Antagonism, indifference, and a ghetto mentality constantly threaten these Christian communities. Yet since the justification of the godless is at the very heart of the Christian faith, the atheism and critique of religion which accompany socialism cannot be obstacles to a realistic evaluation of its aims and practices.

Christians are obligated by their faith not to concentrate exclusively on what does not yet exist or on what they must reject in their context. The freedom of faith also includes the freedom to cooperate. For Christians under socialist regimes this is an immensely difficult task, because Christianity is still dismissed as a vestige of class society. To give the church any independent power to shape society would be incompatible with the leadership of the working class and the role of the Communist Party. Still, there are opportunities for Christians under socialism to be present at the bleeding points of their commonwealth without identifying fully with the self-styled progress made towards the classless society. Christians can express the primacy of compassion, of love for the enemy, of reconciliation, and of an eschatological view of history as aspects of their faith which are as essential as participation in the building up of a new and better society. Opportunities also exist to help free their fellow-citizens from socialist provincialism and obsession with one particular model of society, thus aiding them to become more open to different situations and struggles in the world.

In earlier chapters we touched on some of the tasks facing Christians in the Third World. As higher energy prices and heavy borrowing threaten countries in Latin America, Africa, and Asia with more poverty and instability, the

Polish strikers meet at the Gdansk shipyards, August 1980

social and political tasks of Christians there become even
more pronounced. Those on the outside should be cautious
about deploring the conditions in such lands. It is popular
among some Western journalists to dwell on the joylessness
and drabness of these Third World societies, the inequities
of their one-party governments, their continuing economic
headaches, inefficiency, rampant mismanagement. But
wherever fewer people are starving, wherever slums are
being erased and illiteracy attacked, wherever racism is condemned, wherever day-care centers and health clinics are
being built and the infant mortality rate is being lowered,
these positive developments must be lifted up. Rationing of
food and shortages of consumer goods are not necessarily
an indication that a society is developing in the wrong direction. Production is, after all, a means to an end, not the end
in itself.

The crux for Third World nations is to participate in an
economic system which produces enough to feed the
hungry, house the homeless, provide hospital care, and
bring joy into more lives. Central to this is the question of
income distribution. The words spoken by the Old Testament prophets in the face of rampant inequities in Israelite
society hundreds of years before Christ find an echo in

underdeveloped countries today, where a small minority is very well off and the majority lives in grinding poverty.

But those prophetic words apply equally to the affluent nations. There must be modifications in the way capitalism and the international economic order operate if they are to meet biblical criteria of justice and righteousness. The lower classes, the marginal people, the unemployed all have reason to repeat the words of Jeremiah 22:13:

> Woe to him who builds his house by unrighteousness,
>   and his upper rooms by injustice;
> who makes his neighbour serve him for nothing,
>   and does not give him his wages.

Welfare for all is not an optional extra for biblically serious Christians. It is an essential which must be supported at all times and everywhere.

Even so brief an account as we have sketched in this chapter of the differing situations Christians face in the world today can seem far too overwhelming and complex to confront. How can Christians who recognize the diminished influence of the church in contemporary societies East and West do anything in such a world but pray "Thy kingdom come?" Is it even possible to speak of *working* for the coming of that kingdom in any relevant fashion? How can we fulfil, in explicit ways, our responsibility to build a human community which is as peaceful, loving, and hopeful as possible? Adhering to a party and voting intelligently is not enough. Uttering vague, impersonal, and uncommitted abstractions will not do.

In our concluding section we shall look at "people-politics" — as not so much a Christian Manifesto as a biblically grounded sensitivity to some of the opportunities Christians can seize for making the messianic power of the risen Christ work in a world that has too often seen that power placed at the disposal of those who would oppress their fellow humans for their own gain.

People-politics

Political power, used and abused, is a universal phenomenon. When the Greek philosopher Aristotle observed, several centuries before Christ, that "man is a political animal," he was only making explicit what is apparent no matter where you look in the historical record, including the Bible. The Old Testament Books of Kings are full of political struggles and power plays. The crucifixion of Jesus followed a trial that moved back and forth between the religious and political authorities in Jerusalem. The Apostle Paul lived and preached and traveled against the background of the political might of the Roman Empire, whose citizenship he proudly claimed.

Though many of Paul's letters to young churches are concerned with issues of doctrine and practice, he also reflected about matters which we would call political. The word "power" (in Greek, *exousia*) appears in a famous passage in his letter to the Christians in Rome. "Every person must submit to the supreme powers," he wrote. Why? "There is no power but by act of God, and the existing powers are instituted by him" (Romans 13:1).

Paul had been born into a theocratic society. His age was one in which government was seen as being under the immediate direction of God or several gods. As a Jew Paul knew that the power of the monarchs in Israel and Judah had been ordained by God himself. But Paul also considered the Roman Empire a theocratic state. He appreciated being a citizen of that society. Rome was an empire of many gods and lords, where divine influence was felt in every sphere of life. The Romans could understand Paul's language when he talked about the power to rule as something divinely instituted. Out of his heart came the conviction that "the authorities are in God's service, and to these duties they devote their energies" (Romans 13:6). The key word in a theocratic social and political structure is *obedience*. It was thus beyond the realm of Paul's experience to develop a political theology of liberation.

Quite a different perspective on power is found in the final book of the New Testament. Like other so-called apocalyptic literature of its period, the Book of Revelation speaks about history within history. It soars into the realm of visions and dreams. In vivid, picturesque language it tells of a hideous beast with ten horns and seven heads who rises out of the sea. The dragon conferred on this beast his power and rule and great authority, and the whole world went after the beast in wondering admiration. People worshiped the beast, chanting: "Who is like the Beast? Who can fight against it?" (Revelation 13:1-4). The beast is anti-God. When it refuses to submit to God's rule, all God seems to be able to do is impose a time limit on the manifestations of its dazzling power.

A second beast, with two horns like a lamb's, exercises power in a more subtle fashion. Yet it displays another frightful aspect of the dragon power: it imposes a totalitarian ideology on the world society. "It causes all, both small and great, both rich and poor, both free and slave, to be marked on the right hand or the forehead, so that no one can buy or sell unless he has the mark" (Revelation 13:16-17).

There is only one alternative to the power politics of both theocratic and totalitarian societies, and that is people-politics. But such a politics is extremely difficult to put into practice. Realism about just how difficult it is lies behind Jesus' words of commission to his disciples: "I send you out as sheep in the midst of wolves; so be wise as serpents and innocent as doves" (Matthew 10:16). Involvement in people-politics requires of Christians both a "dove ethics" and a "serpent politics." If you turn the other cheek, you must know what you are doing. You should not subject yourself to brutal forces totally unprepared. When you give away your coat and your shirt, you must know why you do it — and it ought not to be out of mere helplessness.

The "serpent" in Jesus' figure of speech here is not the symbol of deception, craftiness, and seduction as in the temptation in Eden, but the model of discretion, prudence, and wisdom. On a mission among wolves, shrewd political strategy is called for. But serpent politics without dove ethics is a politics of perverse and destructive power. Conversely, dove ethics without serpent politics is weak and foolish. When dove ethics is strengthened by serpent politics and serpent politics informed by dove ethics, Christians are prepared for a tough engagement in people-politics against power-politics.

But, as we have been emphasizing, people-politics requires great faith, discernment, ingenuity, and endurance. Jesus' brief life on earth did not institute a paradise here. To the consternation of many of his followers, who expected a utopia just around the corner, it brought him straight to death on a cross. Through him, the reign of God was carried into the demonic kingdom, but it was not universally and finally extended. Christ established signs that his kingdom had drawn near, that the life-and-death struggle against the powers and authorities of this age had begun.

Involvement in people-politics is not a call to do more than that, but neither is it permission to settle for less. Instead of leaving the demonic kingdom in peace, Christians, as witnesses of the resurrection of their Lord and instruments of his Holy Spirit, are called to attack it everywhere. Not all Christians must become committed revolutionaries, or socialists, or even political activists. But all can and must work for the breaking in of the kingdom in one way or another.

Yet even this is too much a one-sided appeal to the *individual* conscience and to *personal* political initiative. It does not yet lead to a genuine democracy. We need to be caught up *together* in people-politics; we need to work together at increasing our faith, our discernment, our ingenuity, our endurance. People-politics is a risky affair, demanding constant mutual correction as we seek to operate in that uncertain political realm between Romans 13 and Revelation 13.

There will always be Christians around who are ready to quote Scripture against the disturbances with which people-politics threatens the status quo. "Render to Caesar the things that are Caesar's, and to God the things that are God's" (Mark 12:17), they will say, arguing for quietism as not only a necessity but a positive Christian virtue. Paul's admonition that slaves should "be obedient to those who are your earthly masters, with fear and trembling, in singleness of heart, as to Christ" (Ephesians 6:5) is the sort of exhortation which, wrenched out of its context in a theocratic culture, can be used to defend all sorts of subtle forms of modern slavery in many racist societies.

When people cry, "Who is like the Beast? Who can fight it?", people-politics seems impossible. And there is no doubt about the awesome might of this beast, which is allowed to wage war on God's people and defeat them and which is granted authority over every tribe and people, language and nation (Revelation 13:7). Events in the memory of most people alive today seem to fulfil its dreadful promise — the holocaust of Jews under Nazi terror, the genocide carried out by the murderous Pol Pot regime in Kampuchea, the brutal invasion of Afghanistan by the Soviets, the slaughter of political enemies and innocent people — often in a fit of rage — by Idi Amin of Uganda . . . the list could be extended almost indefinitely.

The second beast, too, is a threat to people-politics. This beast is the performer of economic miracles, the bearer of the orderly society. It boasts of spectacular increases in per capita income, though the masses remain destitute, propped up by the promises of those who bear the mark of the beast that a happy world society is just around the corner. Dissidents pay for their protest with imprisonment, torture, and death.

Not all politics that talks about "people" is people-politics. Not long after the Russian Revolution the notion of people's involvement in that new society became dubious. The vanguard of professional revolutionaries took over in the name of the proletariat, but the vast working class was soon as alienated from the leaders in the Kremlin as it had been from the czars in their imperial splendour. Countries like China may take on the name "People's Republic" and claim that "Serve the people" is the highest command. But in what sense, to what degree, do the nearly one billion Chinese serve one another as dignified human beings? Juan Péron may have established a "populist" regime in Argentina, but how can one speak of people-politics in a country where the generals have taken over and allow rightist and leftist factions to murder each other and scores of innocent people in the process? In the West, as we saw in the preceding section, churches operate in the mezzo-structure of society, not really able to come to grips with the crucial issues of power and decision-making, not sharing in national and international responsibility. Here, too, people-politics can become a mere self-deluding fad.

True people-politics will be sensitive to the superfluous manipulation of the consumers by advertising, to the squandering of irreplaceable resources, to garbage in the streets of big cities, to the jewels and luxuries of the "jet set," to vast fortunes drenched in blood in the security of numbered Swiss bank accounts, to military expansionism that claims to be defending the "free world." A people-politics worthy of its intentions will denounce all the false gods of power, of national security, of wealth, of order, of democracy. It will not allow us to forget the accumulation of land by the oligarchies of Latin America, or the dead bodies in clandestine cemeteries, or the genocidal armies in the countries of Africa, or the napalm and poison dropped on the people and crops of poor countries who happen to be pawns in a global power struggle.

Genuine people-politics is very specific in talking about enormous disparities in salary scales, availability of education, and ratios of the number of qualified medical personnel to the population. It attacks the insatiable hunger for profit of individuals and corporations. It points out the lie

Salgado Jr

in the pious claims of capitalist societies to share the wealth and in the myth of charismatic leadership in underdeveloped nations.

People-politics is not phony populism or folk wisdom. It works with its own blueprint for a better society, improving and correcting that model according to harmful or promising developments in the nation. It feels free to borrow from the basic principles and daily experiences of liberal-democratic, socialist, and Communist systems. It rejects the arguments of petty partisan politics or governments which claim to impose "law and order" for the common good but which exist only for their own purposes and stifle any initiative or protest on the part of their citizens.

Every political slogan, concern, intervention, promise must be carefully examined and reexamined. As an example, take the five principles of "Pancasila," which guide Indonesian society — belief in one God, humanity, the unity of Indonesia, guided democracy, and social justice. People politics asks pointed questions about this. Does Pancasila mean that Buddhists, agnostics, and atheists can at best be only second-class citizens? Who guarantees that this Indonesian unity is not achieved at the expense of humanity? To what extent is democracy "guided" — and by whom? What does social justice mean when thousands of political dissidents languish and die in remote prisons without trial and millions of inhabitants live at or barely above the poverty line?

In particular people-politics demystifies the magic word "socialism," recognizing its many ambiguous meanings. Socialism may be practiced not in the name of and by the people themselves, but apart from them by a new privileged élite. Human dignity can be sacrificed, creativity and freedom smothered, by bowing down to the idol of socialism. Socialism as a mere end is in flagrant contradiction to socialism as a possible means of enhancing the humanization of society.

Christians who are engaged in people-politics can remind their fellow human beings that the mighty principalities and powers will never be totally defeated until the end of this world. Sustained by their faith in the victory of the crucified and risen Lord, they whisper in the ears of their sometimes-faltering fellow citizens that their common people-politics is the next-to-the-last struggle before God's rule over humanity is inaugurated.

Who can hesitate or refuse to be counted with the people in this kind of politics? As ever more men and women are drawn into active and meaningful involvement in local, national, and international issues, their personal doubts, dangerous ignorance, wavering commitments, phony arguments, pious restraint, blind attachment to the past, and overwhelming sense of helplessness fade. And on the faces of Christians one can discover that they have caught a glimpse of the resurrection of the dead.

That is why they act as they do.

The last section of this chapter draws on C. S. Song's unpublished lecture, "The Rat and the Ox: Rethinking Christian Power Ethic", in which he develops the ideas of people politics versus power politics and of a dove ethics combined with serpent politics. This lecture was presented to the consultation "Towards Ecumenical Ethics in the Eighties", at Bossey, Switzerland, in July 1980.

Appendices

SOME KEY DATES IN THE COMMUNIST WORLD

1818-1883	Karl Marx
1847-1952	The Communist League
1848	Publication of the *Communist Manifesto*
1862-1876	The First International (Working Men's Association)
1889-1915	The Second International
1917	The Russian October Revolution
1919-1943	The Third International (COMINTERN)
1920	Founding of the French Communist Party
1921	Founding of the Chinese and Italian Communist Parties
1924	Death of Vladimir I. Lenin
1926-1937	Prison Notes of Antonio Gramsci
1947-1956	Communist Information Bureau (COMINFORM)
1949	The Chinese Revolution
1950-1953	The Korean War
1953	Death of Joseph Stalin
1956	Soviet Invasion of Hungary
1958-1960	The Great Leap Forward (China)
1962	The Cuban Missile Crisis
1964	Death of Maurice Thorez and Palmiro Togliatti
1966-1969	The Great Proletarian Cultural Revolution China
1968	Soviet Invasion of Czechoslovakia
1970-1973	Chile under the Salvador Allende Regime
1973	Unification of North and South Vietnam
1976	Death of Mao Tse-Tung
Dec. 1979	Soviet Invasion of Afghanistan

MEMBERSHIP OF THE PRINCIPAL
COMMUNIST PARTIES IN THE WORLD

	Estimated Population	Party Membership
People's Republic of China	908,000,000	35,000,000
USSR	258,930,000	16,500,000
Rumania	21,855,000	2,740,000
Poland	34,850,200	2,573,000
German Democratic Republic	16,757,857	2,000,000
North Korea	16,650,000	2,000,000
Italy	57,070,000	1,715,922
Yugoslavia	21,968,000	1,623,612
Vietnam	46,523,000	1,553,000
Czechoslovakia	15,030,583	1,473,112
Bulgaria	8,761,000	817,000
Hungary	10,684,000	765,566
France	53,196,000	680,000
Cuba	9,464,000	202,807

Observations and comments

Many of these statistics are taken from *The Europa Yearbook: A World Survey 1979*. Most of the estimated population figures are dated January 1, 1978, though some figures go back to mid-1976 and mid-1977. The figure for the People's Republic of China is a 1980 estimate. No figures for Communist Party membership in countries such as Spain, Angola, Mozambique, and Guinea are provided.

In Communist countries in the world, totalling approximately 1,381,000,000 inhabitants, not more than approximately 68 million people

— or five per cent of the total population — belong to a Communist Party. In Cuba only 2 per cent of the population are members of the Partido Communisto Cubano.

To maintain control, Communist Parties tightly restrict their membership. In the Soviet Union a candidate must have been a member of Komsomol, the Communist youth organization, be recommended by three people who have been members for three years, and pass other screening procedures, including serving a year on probation. USSR workers make up 42 per cent of the membership of the Party; collective farmers 13.6 per cent.

Of the 193 million Soviet citizens who were 18 and older in 1979, only 16 million — or 9 per cent — were party members. (In Khrushchev's day the figure was 6 per cent.) Except for a few scientific administrators, virtually every responsible official in the Soviet governnment is a party member. Although it is impossible to separate party from government, one point is clear: the party makes policy.

At the top of the party pyramid is the Central Committee, whose 287 members include the most powerful individuals in the nation. Fourteen of the "most equal among the equals" on the Central Committee constitute the policy-setting Politburo, which has been carefully controlled for most of the past 16 years by Leonid Brezhnev and his circle.

The Central Committee chooses the General Secretary of the Communist Party, the most powerful position in the nation. Decisions of the Politburo are adopted and carried out by an elaborate system of local, regional, and national governments whose apex is the Supreme Soviet, an elected parliament. This body consists of the Soviet of the Union, composed of 750 members, each of whom represents a district of about 350,000; and the Soviet of the nationalities, also composed of 750 members, including 32 from each of the 15 republics.

The Supreme Soviet, which meets twice a year in the Kremlin, can raise and debate issues, and hence may affect the decisions of the Central Committee. Officials claim that the general attitudes of a newly elected Supreme Soviet sometimes influence the Politburo. But the legislators would never advocate a position known to be at variance with the views of the leadership. Indeed, members of the Presidium of the Supreme Soviet often also belong to the Central Committee.

The Soviet masses who are not party members can work through local organizations, such as trade "unions" and newspapers, to influence policy; but these too are controlled by the party. The Supreme Soviet is elected every five years; there is just one slate of candidates: the party's. In March 1979, when the Supreme Soviet was last chosen, 99.99% of the eligible voters were said to have cast their ballots. Tass, the Soviet news agency, declared: "By their unanimous voting for the candidates, the Soviet people expressed complete support for the domestic and foreign policies of the Communist Party and the Soviet state."

Constitutions of the Communist Party-States, edited by Jan F. Triska (The Hoover Institution on War, Revolution and Peace, Stanford University), contains the texts of the constitutions (fundamental laws) adopted by each of the Communist party-states, as well as amendments. The texts are either official English translations or the most authoritative unofficial translations available.

Total World Population   4,200,000,000

Christians in the World   984,000,000

Total Population of Countries
Under Communist Regimes   1,381,000,000

Total of Communist Party Members
(approx.).   76,000,000

APPENDIX III

THE WEALTH PER INHABITANT OF EACH COUNTRY

In 1978 15% of the world's population shared 60% of world revenue; 20% shared only 2% of world revenue.

Kuwait: $15,000 per person per year
USA: $9,700 per person per year
Bangladesh: $90 per person per year

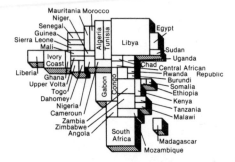

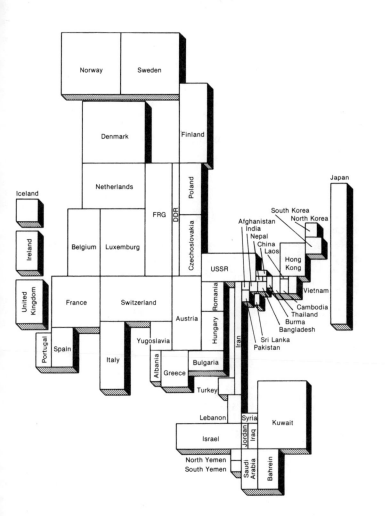
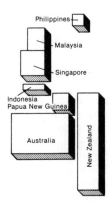

Norway

Sweden

Denmark

Finland

Iceland

Netherlands

Poland

Japan

Ireland

FRG

DDR

Czechoslovakia

Afghanistan
India
Nepal
China
Laos

South Korea
North Korea

Belgium

Luxemburg

Hong Kong

United Kingdom

France

Switzerland

USSR

Vietnam

Romania

Cambodia
Thailand
Burma
Bangladesh

Austria

Hungary

Iran

Sri Lanka
Pakistan

Portugal

Spain

Yugoslavia

Italy

Albania

Greece

Bulgaria

Turkey

Lebanon

Syria

Kuwait

Israel

Jordan

Iraq

North Yemen
South Yemen

Saudi Arabia

Bahrein

Philippines

Malaysia

Singapore

Indonesia
Papua New Guinea

Australia

New Zealand

APPENDIX IV

A SELECTION OF CLASSICS AND CURRENT BOOKS FOR FURTHER READING

Marxism

Fromm, Erich. *Marx's Concept of Man*. New York: Frederick Ungar Publ. Co., 1961.

A provocative view of Marx, stressing his humanist philosophy and challenging both Soviet distortion and Western ignorance of his basic thinking. With a translation from Marx's "Economic and Philosophical Manuscripts," by T.B. Bottomore.

Gramsci, Antonio. *Selections from the Prison Notebooks*. Ed. and tr. by Q. Hoare and G.N. Smith. New York: International Publishers, 1971.

Studies in history, politics, and philosophy, written by the imprisoned Italian Communist leader between 1929 and 1935. Among the most creative Marxist writings ever penned.

Marx, Karl. *Capital: A Critical Analysis of Capitalist Production*. Moscow: Progress Publishers, 1965. 3 vols.

Marx, Karl and Engels, Friedrich. *On Religion*. New York: Schocken, 1964.

A selection of the major statements on religion found in their works.

Marx, Karl and Engels, Friedrich. *Selected Works*. New York: International Publishing Co., 1968.

Lenin, Vladimir. *Selected Works*. New York: International Publishing Co., 1971.

Stalin, Iosif. *Selected Writings*. Westport, CT: Greenwood, 1942.

Maoism

Christianity and the New China. Vol. I: Theological Implications of the New China. Vol. II: Christian Faith and the Chinese Experience. South Pasadena, CA: Ecclesia Publications, William Carey Library, 1976.

Contains papers and reports presented at an Ecumenical Seminar, held in Basted, Sweden, in early 1974, and from an Ecumenical Colloquium, held in Louvain, Belgium, in September the same year. Two ecumenical meetings, in the last three decades, representing the work of nearly a hundred Protestant and Catholic scholars facing the far-reaching implications of the vast Chinese experiment in social engineering, and reflecting an attitude of selfappraisal and a common search for theological understanding.

Mao Tse-Tung. *Selected Works*. Peking: Foreign Language Press, 1965. 4 vols.

Schramm, Stuart R. *The Political Thought of Mao Tsetung*. New York: Praeger Publishers, 1969.

A thorough examination of the development of Mao's thought, his road to power, and his own contribution to Marxist-Leninist theory. Throughout the book the question is posed: how far was Communism an end for Mao and how far a means to China's resurgence?

Snow, Edgar. *The Long Revolution*. New York: Vintage Books, 1971.

An account of the author's last trip to China in 1971, when he once again held long and candid talks with Mao, Chou En-Lai, and hosts of other Chinese. Among Snow's other well-known books are *Red Star Over China* and *Red China Today*.

Terrill, Ross. *The Future of China After Mao*. New York: Dell Publishing Co., 1978.

A clear picture of the chain of events during the last decade. The author analyzes the new balance of power in China, with the army, the youth, and the new consumers all making their demands increasingly felt. What old patterns will continue and what new ones evolve?

Anti-Communism

Anatomy of Anti-Communism. A report prepared for the Peace Education Division of the American Friends Service Committee. New York: Hill and Wang, 1969.

The book shows how anti-Communism has become a political strategy that often utilizes the fear of Communism as a camouflage for conservative and even reactionary politics.

Evans, G. Russell. *Apathy, Apostasy and Apostles*. A Study of the History and Activities of the National Council of Churches of Christ in the USA with Sidelights on its Ally: The World Council of Churches. New York: Vantage Press, 1973.

Claimed to be a "fascinating and controversial analysis... a penetrating exposure of the shocking, radical, secular and revolutionary activities of Protestantism's super church council."

Lefever, Ernst W. *Amsterdam to Nairobi: The World Council of Churches and the Third World*. Washington, DC: Georgetown University, Ethics and Public Policy Center, 1979.

WCC thinking is, according to the author, a revolutionary doctrine indistinguishable from current Marxist concepts. The Western churches, in their death agonies, are spreading the cause of their own sickness — the politicization of religion — to their healthy offspring in the developing world.

Wages of Sin: The World Council of Churches Unmasked. A documented report from the research staff of the Church League of America, Wheaton, IL, 1979.

"The WCC is definitely biased in favour of Communism and Communists. The documents we have examined and brought to your attention in the preceding pages show this to be a fact."

Wurmbrand, Richard. *In God's Underground*. London: Allen, 1968.

One of the numerous books of a once-imprisoned Rumanian pastor which have been widely sold and read.

Christian-Marxist Dialogue

A Christian's Handbook on Communism. New York: National Council of the Churches of Christ in the U.S.A. The Committee on World Literacy and Christian Literature. Third Revised and Enlarged Edition, 1962.

A description of Communist theory and practice and an exposition of the nature of the Christian faith and its expression through the church. Leaders in church circles and educational institutions gave counsel, information, and new insights during the preparation of this handbook. Like the book by Donald Evans (see below) it reflects a North American position twenty years ago.

Dean, Thomas: *Post-Theistic Thinking: The Marxist-Christian Dialogue in Radical Perspective*. Philadelphia: Temple University Press, 1979.

No longer theological in any sense, Dean's perspective on contemporary Christianity in relation to Marxism draws on recent theological movements to offer a positive, finitist interpretation of traditional theological positions such as man's sense of limits, the reality of transcendence, and the working of history in the Christian tradition.

Evans, Donald: *Communist Faith and Christian Faith*. London: SCM Press, 1965.

This book was originally adopted as a report of the Committee on Christian Faith of the United Church of Canada and given general approval by its General Assembly. Although now out of date, it is one of the very few good and reliable manuals on the subject ever published in English. Each chapter closes with a commentary, discussing disagreements and agreements with Communism and Christian options.

Garaudy, Roger. *Marxism in the Twentieth Century*. London: Collins, 1970.

The French philosopher reflects the new spirit that has been alive in Marxist thought in recent years, a reawakening to the essence of Marxism, which restores to human beings both their responsibility for the future and their creative potential. Among his numerous other books, *From Anathema to Dialogue: A Marxist Challenge to the Christian Churches* (1966), was widely circulated.

Lochman, Jan Milic: *Encountering Marx: Bonds and Barriers Between Christians and Marxists*. Philadelphia: Fortress Press, 1977.

Introduces the young Marx, on the basis of papers whose importance has only recently begun to be felt by Christians, although long recognized and suppressed by doctrinaire Marxists. What is the human face of Communism?

Machovec, Milan: *A Marxist Looks at Jesus*. London: Darton, Longman and Todd, 1976.

Both Jesus' and Marx's message have been distorted by Christianity and Communism. Yet Marxism is still a potent ideological force, according to this Czech philosopher. It is Marxists rather than Christians who have respected Jesus' legacy of "longing for redemption and for radical inner change."

Miguez-Bonino, José: *Christians and Marxists: The Mutual Challenge to Revolution*. London: Hodder & Stoughton, 1976.

In Latin America there is cooperation and tension between Christians and Marxists. The latter challenge the bourgeois irresponsibility of many Christians, according to the author; and the Christians challenge the Marxists' naive views of man and of history, not to mention their non-view of God. "Common struggle" and "mutual challenge" are the themes of the book.

Varieties of Christian-Marxist Dialogue. Ed. by Paul Mojzes. A special number of the *Journal of Ecumenical Studies*, Vol. 15, No. 1, Winter 1978.

Contributions by various experts, edited by Prof. Mojzes of Rosemont College in Pennsylvania, who chairs the Task Force on the Christian-Marxist Encounter of Christians Associated for Relationships with Eastern Europe.

Christians for Socialism

Christianity and Socialism. Ed. by Johann-Baptist Metz and Jean-Pierre Jossua. New York: Seabury Press, 1977. (*Concilium*, V. 105).

Offers essentially information and documentation serving to orient readers puzzled by a complex of problems too often discussed within the church only in apologetical and polemical clichés. There are a variety of contributions from Western capitalist, socialist, and Third World countries.

Christians and Socialism. Documentation of the Christian for Socialism Movement in Latin America. Ed. by John Eagleson. Maryknoll, N.Y.: Orbis Books, 1975.

A collection of background documents, draft agendas, "movement hierarchy" dossiers, national reports (Chile, Peru, Puerto Rico, Cuba), convention and post-convention documents during the years 1971-1973.

The Encounter of The Church with Movements of Social Change in Various Cultural Contexts. Part I: Papers from a Seminar in Bossey, Switzerland, Sept. 21-27, 1975. Part II: Papers from a Consultation in Glion, Switzerland, July 4-11, 1976. Geneva: Lutheran World Federation, Dept. of Studies, 1977.

Many papers in this volume deal with the subject of Christianity and socialism in an affirmative way, though the authors are not representative of the movement and the scope of the material is wider, including an attempt to systematize descriptions of the various relations between the churches and various forms of socialism.

Witness of the Gospel in the Struggle for Socialism. Geneva: World Student Christian Federation, 1976.

Contains lectures and reports from the European Student's Conference at Lillehammer, Norway, Sept. 25-30, 1975.

Faith and Order

Lange, Ernest: *And Yet It Moves: Dream and Reality of the Ecumenical Movement.* Belfast: Christian Journals Ltd., 1979.

A thorough analysis of the strengths and weaknesses of the ecumenical movement and a personal account of experience in the service of the ecumenical cause.

One Baptism, One Eucharist and a Mutually Recognized Ministry. Three Agreed Statements. Geneva: WCC, 1975.

Texts designed to help the churches discover their oneness in fellowship with Christ and thus come to live together in unity. The documents are still being revised in further international consultations.

Partners in Life: The Handicapped and the Church. Ed. by Geiko Müller-Fahrenholz. Geneva: WCC, 1979 (Faith and Order Paper No. 89).

The cause of disabled persons is a demand and a challenge to the whole church, to its theology and its worship, to its congregational life and teaching. This book is the beginning of an attempt to discover anew the wholeness of the family of God in and with disabled persons.

Unity in Today's World. Faith and Order Studies on "Unity of the Church — Unity of Humankind." Ed. by Geiko Müller-Fahrenholz. Geneva: WCC, 1978 (Faith and Order Paper No. 88).

Contains the emergence of the study project, a retrospect of motives and themes leading to the emergence of the present theme, an analysis of contributions from study groups and conferences, and ten individual reactions and comments.

Programme to Combat Racism

Heuvel, Albert van den: *Shalom and Combat: A Personal Struggle Against Racism*. Geneva: WCC, 1979 (Risk Book Series).

A penetrating analysis of how the ecumenical movement has slowly come to grips with the evil of racism. Descriptions of the controversy around the WCC's Special Fund to Combat Racism provide a backdrop to what is essentially a personal confession.

Rogers, Barbara: *Race: No Peace Without Justice*. Geneva: WCC, 1980.

A critical account of the world consultation on racism held in June 1980, and its meaning for the churches.

The Slant of the Pen: Racism in Children's Books. Ed. by Roy Preiswerk. Geneva: WCC, 1980.

This is the full report and other documents of a consultation jointly sponsored by the WCC Office of Education and the Programme to Combat Racism at Arnoldshain, Fed. Rep. of Germany, in October 1978.

World Council of Churches' Statements and Actions on Racism 1948-1979. Ed. by Ans J. van der Bent. Geneva: WCC, 1979 (Programme to Combat Racism).

Contains, besides a collection of ecumenical statements on racism and the struggle against it, a chronological record of how the WCC has faced ethnic tensions and racial conflicts since 1948.

Christianity, Religions, and the World

Faith and Science in an Unjust World. Report of the World Council of Churches' Conference on Faith, Science and the Future, Massachusetts

Institute of Technology, Cambridge, USA, 12-24 July 1979. Vol.1: Plenary Presentations, ed. by Roger L.Shinn; Vol. 2: Reports and Recommendations, ed. by Paul Abrecht. Geneva: WCC, 1980.

Among the many other documents in these two volumes are individual presentations and reports of discussion on the theme of "a just, participatory, and sustainable society."

Faith in the Midst of Faiths. Reflections on Dialogue in Community. Ed. by S.J. Samartha. Geneva: WCC, 1977.

The official report of a theological consultation at Chiang Mai, Thailand, in April 1977, organized by the WCC's sub-unit on Dialogue with People of Living Faiths and Ideologies.

Guidelines on Dialogue with People of Living Faiths and Ideologies. Geneva: WCC, 1979.

The statement adopted at Chiang Mai (see previous title) was received by the WCC Central Committee in 1977. This booklet contains the statement, revised in the light of responses received from the churches, which forms the theological basis for the guidelines that follow.

Santa Ana, Julio de. *Good News to the Poor. The Challenge of the Poor in the History of the Church*. Geneva: WCC, 1977 (Commission on the Churches' Participation in Development).

The first volume in a trilogy on "The Church and the Poor," focusing on the challenge of the poor to the church, as felt by Christian communities during the first four centuries after Christ and again during the late Middle Ages.

Separation Without Hope? Essays on the Relation Between the Church and the Poor During the Industrial Revolution and the Western Colonial Expansion. Geneva: WCC, 1978 (CCPD).

The second volume of the trilogy on "The Church and the Poor," covering the period from 1800-1914.

Towards a Church of the Poor. The Work of an Ecumenical Group on the Church and the Poor. Geneva: WCC, 1980 (CCPD).

This third volume of the trilogy on "The Church and the Poor" stresses that development is not *for* the poor, but can be achieved *by* them and *with* them when they become full participants in the processes which lead to justice and liberation.

Violence, Nonviolence and the Struggle for Social Justice. A Statement Commended by the Central Committee of the WCC, August 1973, for Study, Comment and Action. Geneva: WCC, 1973.

Printed in Switzerland by Corbaz S.A., Montreux